A COLLECTION OF
Indo - global recipes

BOOK 2 CURRIES, STARTERS
& STAPLES

NewDelhi • London

BLUEROSE PUBLISHERS
India | U.K.

Copyright © Ira Ghosh 2025

All rights reserved by author. No part of this publication may be reproduced, stored in a retrieval system or transmitted in any form or by any means, electronic, mechanical, photocopying, recording or otherwise, without the prior permission of the author. Although every precaution has been taken to verify the accuracy of the information contained herein, the publisher assumes no responsibility for any errors or omissions. No liability is assumed for damages that may result from the use of information contained within.

BlueRose Publishers takes no responsibility for any damages, losses, or liabilities that may arise from the use or misuse of the information, products, or services provided in this publication.

For permissions requests or inquiries regarding this publication, please contact:

BLUEROSE PUBLISHERS
www.BlueRoseONE.com
info@bluerosepublishers.com
+91 8882 898 898
+4407342408967

ISBN: 978-93-6452-606-7

Cover design: Yash Singhal
Typesetting: Namrata Saini

First Edition: January 2025

Dedication

I dedicate this book to my late husband Ashis Bindu Ghosh. When we married, I could barely cook! However, my culinary abilities grew and flourished through his constant encouragement and support (and unfailing good humour at some of my less successful creations). His career enabled us to live in different countries and experience and appreciate different cultures. Much later, after I had accumulated my varied collection of recipes from around the world, he encouraged me to share them through their publication. He was instrumental in getting the first version of my recipe collection into a publishable form. If it were not for his hard work, support, and encouragement, this book would not exist, and I would not have been able to share my recipe collection with you.

I also dedicate this book to my mother Ratnavali Baruah who was a very good cook and had some fantastic recipes. She however, never had any set formula. Before my marriage my mother always worried about my lack of culinary ability!

Additionally, I dedicate this book to my grandmother Pragna Sundari Devi who was the first person to author a series of systematic cookbooks in Bengali extending to several volumes. Her books were my constant reference abroad, from which I learnt my basics.

TABLE OF CONTENTS

Introduction 1
Weights, Measures, And Temperatures 3

NON-VEGETARIAN CURRIES 7
Sinhalese Fish And Vegetable Dry Curry 9
Burmese Fish Curry 10
Steamed Fish Burmese Style 11
Fish Sas (Parsi Fish Curry) 12
Khorisa (Assamese Bamboo Pickle) And Fish Curry 13
Chilli Fish A La Bengal (I) 14
Chilli Fish A La Bengal (II) 15
Bengali Chilli Fish (III) 16
Fish Jhaal – Chilli Fish (IV) 17
Ma's Cabbage And Fish Curry 18
Coconut Fish 19
Yogurt Fish 20
Green Coriander Fish Curry 21
Tomato Fish 23
Masala (Spiced) Fish 24
Sorsé (Mustard) Fish 25
Hilsa (Shad) With Mustard, Coconut And Poppyseed 26
Fish Jhole 27
Chanchra Or Bengali Dry Vegetable And Fish Head Curry 29
Malaysian Lobster Or Prawn Curry (Lobster Rendang) 30
Lau (White Gourd) With Shrimps 32
Shrimp And Cauliflower 33
Mummy's Pumpkin And Prawn Curry 34
Prawns In Daab (Green Coconut) 35
Prawn Curry (I) 36
Prawn Curry (II) 37
Prawns In Coconut Sauce (I) 38
Fish Or Prawns In Coconut Sauce (II) 39
Prawn Curry In Coconut Sauce (III) 40
Quick Prawn Malai (Coconut Milk) Curry (IV) 41

Prawn Malad 42
Prawns And Tomato 43
(Steamed) Mustard Prawns Or Fish 44
Prawns Or Fish In The Oven 46
Shrimp Or Fish In Banana Leaves (Fish Pāturi) 47
Simple Light Prawn Kofta Curry 48
Crab Curry 50
Crab Kofta Curry 52
Goan Chicken Curry 53
Bengali Chicken Curry 54
Thick Chicken Curry 56
Chicken Curry (I) 58
Chicken Curry (II) 59
Chicken Korma (I) 60
Chicken Korma (II) 62
Colonial Chicken And Egg Curry 64
Dum Mutton 65
Mutton Korma 66
Posto (White Poppy Seed) Mutton Curry 68
Mutton Pressure Cooker Curry Or In Daab (Green Coconut) 69
Mutton Curry 71
Saag Meat 72
Goan Liver Curry 74
Lamb Or Beef Mince Kebabs In Yogurt 75
Curried Beef And Pumpkin 76

VEGETARIAN CURRIES AND LENTILS 77

Papaya Dalna 79
Green Papaya Dry Curry 80
Ma's Green Papaya Ghonto Or Dry Curry 81
Cauliflower And Potato Kalia (Bengali) 82
Gujarati Peas And Cauliflower Curry 83
Beet Ghonto (Bengali) 84
Sheem (Broad Beans) Paturi – Bengali 85
Shukto (I) – Bengali Starter 86
Lau (White Gourd) Or Vegetable Shukto (II) 87

Shukto (Iii) As A Variation To (I) Or (Ii) 88
Bengali Labra Or Mixed Vegetable Curry 89
Bengali Vegetable Curry Or Dalna 90
Mixed Vegetables With Mustard And Coconut 92
Vegetable Paturi (Bengali Banana Leaf Wrapped Smoked Vegetable Dry Curry) 93
Methi Aloo (Fenugreek Potatoes) 94
Aloo Bati-Chorchori 95
Ma's Aloo Posto (Potato With Poppy Seed Paste) (I) 96
Potato And Poppy Seed Dry Curry (Aloo Posto) (II) 97
Steamed Potatoes With Poppy Seed Paste (III) 98
Aloo Posto (Potato Poppy Seed Curry) (IV) 99
Hing Aloo-Dum (Potato with Asafœtida) 100
Stellamashi's Sorse Aloo (Potatoes In Mustard Sauce) 101
Mummy's Aloo Dum (Dry Potato Curry) 102
Spicy Brinjal 103
Aubergine (Begun) Kalanji 104
Coconut Brinjal 106
Ma's White Pumpkin (*Chaal Kumra*) Curry 107
Piquant Green Jack Fruit (Enchore) Curry 108
Kanchkala Or Green Banana Curry 109
Mummy's Mowcha Chenchki Or Banana Flower Curry 110
Thore Chenchki 111
Thore Ghonto 112
Spinach With Bori 113
Saag Paneer 114
Kochusaaker Ghonto – Curried Taro (*Lat. Colocasia*) Greens 116
Sorse Sag (Mustard Green) Curry 117
Methisaak (Fenugreek Greens) Fry 118
Chhola Or Whole Brown Pea Curry 119
Channa Or Dry Chickpea Curry (I) 120
Dry Chickpea Curry (II) 121
Pakhi's Rajma 122
Sambhar (With Ready-Mix Powder) 123
Sambhar (With Home-Made Mix Powder) 124
Rasam 125

Rasam With Ready-Mix Powder 126
Bengali Cholar Dal (Bengal Gram) (I) 127
Bengali Cholar Dal (Bengal Gram) (II) 128
Simple Bengali Moong (Yellow) Dal 129
Pakhi's Black Moong -- The Punjabi Style 130
Sweet And Sour Arhar (Toor Gram) Dal 131
Gujarati Arhar (Toor Gram) Dal 132

SOUPS 133

Stock 135
Vegetable Soup 136
Minestrone 137
Borsch or Beetroot Soup (I) 138
Cold Beetroot Soup (II) 139
Beetroot Soup (III) 140
Spinach Soup (I) 141
Spinach Soup With Coriander (II) 142
Cold Cucumber Soup (I) 143
Cold Cucumber Soup (II) 144
Cold Cucumber Soup (III) 145
Potato Soup (I) 146
Potato, Cheese, Capsicum Soup (II) 147
Tomato Soup (I) 148
Tomato Soup (II) 149
Basil And Tomato Soup 151
Green Pea Soup 152
Corn Soup 153
Bean Soups 154
Black Bean Soup 155
Red Bean Soup 156
Soya Bean Soup 157
Baked Bean Soup 158
Lentil Or *Dal* Soup 159
Green *Moong (Dal)* Soup (From Leftovers) 160
Mulligatawny Soup 161
Chicken And Corn Soup (I) 163

Chicken And Corn Soup (II) 164
Chinese Chicken And Noodle Soup (I) 165
Chinese Chicken And Noodle Soup (II) 166
Chinese Chicken And Vegetable Soup 167
Chinese Sour And Hot Soup 168
Chawan Musi (I) 169
Chawan Musi (II) 170
Simple Japanese Soup 171
Soup With Butter Dumplings 172
Prawn Soup 173
Hungarian Goulash Soup 174
Yahneli Kufte (Armenian) 175
Middle Eastern Chicken And Rice Soup 177
Middle Eastern Mutton Soup 178
Hodge Podge Soup 179
Thick Broth 180
Cold Yogurt Soup 181
Variations of Cold And Hot Soups 182

BREADS AND ROLLS 183

Quick Easy White Bread 185
Bachelor's or Students' Easy Bread 186
Bread Rolls 187
Beigli (Sesame Roll) 188
Ice Box Or Refrigerator Rolls 189
Hot Rolls 190
Simple Bread Rolls/Sticks And Pizza Dough 191
Methi Paratha 192
Baking Powder Parathas 193
Easy Parathas 194
Egg Parathas 195
Tandoori Roti 196
Gujarati Muslim Chapattis 197
Pea Kochuri 198

RICE … **199**

Coconut Rice … 201
Japanese Rice … 202
Quick Risotto … 203
Simple Gujarati Pulao … 205
Gujarati Kitchri … 206
Khitchri The Parsi Way … 207
Bora Biriani … 208
Fish Biryani … 210

Glossary … 212
Alphabetical List of Recipes … 217

INTRODUCTION

"*A Collection of Indo Global Recipes*", as the name suggests, is a collection of recipes that is influenced by my Indian background, as well as being the result of spending many years in different countries where my husband's job took me. While abroad, I actively participated in various international groups and made friends with people from many different countries.

I do not consider myself a great cook! However, I was always interested in collecting and devising new recipes and trying them out on friends and family. Their enthusiastic responses indicated that I must have been doing something right! Hoping that others might wish to enjoy the pleasure of cooking and experimenting with recipes from around the world with minimum effort, I decided to publish my collection. In addition to many of the Indian recipes I inherited or learned from my family, I have been building this collection since my husband's first international posting in 1967. I have also added to the collection recipes that I invented over this time. I have tried out all the recipes, and this book is the result of my explorations, collection, and experimentation. Many of the recipes have familiar names, but often prepared differently by various cooks. I tried to simplify each recipe, and in doing so built up a collection that is user-friendly. In a few recipes I could not forgo the temptation of using "ajinomoto" (MSG; monosodium glutamate) as this was a popular ingredient when I collected the recipes. In the intervening years, it was reputed to be harmful, but recently it has been classified by the U.S. Food and Drug Administration of being safe. However, if there is concern, ajinomoto may be replaced with a pinch of sugar to retain somewhat similar flavour.

I hope my work will be of use to many enthusiastic and curious cooks including the offspring of Indian diaspora living abroad, youthful techies wishing to serve party-fares, connoisseurs researching ethnic cooking, and adventurous cooks wanting to make good, interesting food with ease from diverse recipes. Some of the dishes remain time-consuming, but most can be made with a few quick and easy steps.

This book was a labour of love, and my family encouraged me through the years I took to complete this project. I published the first version of this collection, entitled "*A Collection of Recipes*" in 2012 in one large volume. My husband did the tremendous job of computerization and editing that version. However, before I could publish my book, I needed to first complete another important project. I had taken on the colossal task of editing the multi-volume cookbook in Bengali titled "*Amish O Niramish Ahar*" written by my grandmother Pragna Sundari Devi. My grandmother was the first writer of a systematic cookbook in Bengali. Her volumes were published starting from the year 1900 AD. My re-edited and re-arranged versions were published in 1995, after which I could concentrate on my recipe collection. In the years since I first published my collection, I have received feedback and added to it. It is now timely to re-edit and publish the current collection, but this time as a four-volume set to make it more accessible, user friendly, and with a slight change in title to reflect its roots in both Indian and international cuisines. My son, Dr. Richik Niloy Ghosh, was instrumental in helping me create this new four-volume version.

Many thanks are due to my relations and friends in India and abroad from whom I collected the original recipes, modified versions of which now appear in these pages. I am unable to thank them all individually. As my sources were from many nationalities using various units of measurements (metric, avoirdupois, and cups), I kept the units as were given in the originals. To assist the users, I have appended a conversion table covering the three systems. A glossary has also been added to help the reader to understand unfamiliar terms.

Bon Appétit

Ira Ghosh

29 February 2024

WEIGHTS, MEASURES, and TEMPERATURES

1. SOLID MEASURES

1 kg. (kilogram) = 1,000 gm. (gram) = 2.2 lb. (pound avoirdupois)

1 lb. = 16 oz. (ounce)

(a) Equivalent measures of some commodities

Avoirdupois measure	Commodity	Container equivalent
1 pound	Butter or other fat	2 cups
1 pound	Flour	4 cups
1 pound	Granulated or castor sugar	2 cups
1 pound	Icing or confectioner's sugar	3 cups
1 pound	Brown (moist) sugar	2 cups
1 pound	Golden syrup or treacle	1 cup
1 pound	Rice	2 cups
1 pound	Dried fruit	2 cups
1 pound	Chopped meat (finely packed)	2 cups
1 pound	Lentils or split peas	2 cups
1 pound	Coffee (beans)	2 cups
1 pound	Soft breadcrumbs	4 cups
½ ounce	Flour	1 level tablespoon
1 ounce	Flour	1 heaped tablespoon
1 ounce	Sugar	1 level tablespoon
¾ ounce	Butter	1 tablespoon smoothed off
1 ounce	Golden syrup or treacle	1 tablespoon
1 ounce	Jam or jelly	1 level tablespoon

(b) Dry volume/ weight measures

Container	Container	Volume	Weight
4 teaspoons (tsp.)	1 tablespoon	½ fluid ounce	14.3 grams
2 tablespoons (tblsp.)	⅛ cup	1 fluid ounce	28.6 grams
4 tablespoons	⅓ cup	2 fluid ounces	56.7 grams
5⅓ tablespoons	½ cup	2.6 fluid ounce	75.6 grams
8 tablespoons	½ cup	4 fluid ounces	113.4 grams
12 tablespoons	¾ cup	6 fluid ounces	170 grams (.375 pound)
32 tablespoons	2 cups	16 fluid ounces	453.6 grams (1 Pound)
64 tablespoons	4 cups	32 fluid ounces	907 grams (2 pounds)

2. LIQUID MEASURES

(a) Common usage

Measure	Measure	Measure	Volume
1 cup	8 fluid ounces	½ pint	237 millilitres
2 cups	16 fluid ounces	1 pint	474 millilitres.
4 cups	32 fluid ounces	1 quart	946 millilitres
1 pint	16 fluid ounces	½ quart	473 millilitres
2 pints	32 fluid ounces	1 quart	0.964 litres.
4 quarts	128 fluid ounces	1 gallon	3.784 litres
8 quarts	One peck		
4 pecks	One bushel		
dash	Less than ¼ teaspoon		

(b) Small quantities

1 teaspoon (US)	1/6 ounce	4.93 millilitres
1 tablespoon (US)	0.5 ounce	3 teaspoons
1 teaspoon (UK)	1.2 teaspoon (US)	6.16 millilitres
1 tablespoon (UK)	1.2 tablespoon (US)	18.48 millilitres
1 dessert spoon (UK)	2.4 teaspoons	12.32 millilitres
1 dash	~ ⅛ teaspoon	~ 0.6 millilitres

3. APPROXIMATE OVEN TEMPERATURES

Oven	Gas Regulo	Electricity	
		°F	°C
Cool	0 - ½	225 – 250	107 – 121
Very Slow	½ - 1	250 – 275	121 -135
Slow	1 - 2	275 – 300	135 – 149
Very Moderate	2 – 3	300 – 350	149 – 177
Moderate	4	375	190
Moderately Hot	5	400	204
Hot	6 – 7	435 – 450	218 – 233
Very Hot	8 - 9	475 - 500	245 - 260

Ovens might somewhat differ in their specifications.

NON-VEGETARIAN CURRIES

SINHALESE FISH AND VEGETABLE DRY CURRY

2-3 tblsp. oil	250 gm. dry fish or prawns
2 large green peppers, seeded, cut in 4 and soaked in salt water	10-12 cloves garlic whole
250 gm. small whole red onions peeled	½ tsp. turmeric
1½ tblsp. coriander powder	500 gm. long brinjal cut in 4 and rubbed with salt and turmeric
1" piece cinnamon stick	1½ cumin powder
Salt to taste	Dry seeded red chillis to taste
1 tblsp. sugar	1 coconut – thick and thin extracts amounting to 2 cups
1 tblsp. mustard paste	2 oz. red vinegar

Method

Heat oil. Fry fish, peppers, garlic, brinjals and onions – in this order. Drain and put aside after frying each item. Mix all the rest of the ingredients except vinegar, sugar, and mustard paste, with coconut milk, salt, and boil. When milk starts boiling add all fried items and simmer by lowering heat till gravy is thick. At the last minute add a mixture of vinegar, sugar, and mustard paste. Stir well. Take off fire and serve with steamed rice.

(This curry is supposed to be very hot and red and, to get this effect at least 15 dry red chilies should be used. To balance the hotness, vinegar and sugar are added. However, if your palate can not take it, do without the chilies or, add a small quantity. To get the red colour, use either tomato puree or a little food colouring usually used for Tandoori chicken)

Variation:

Instead of coconut milk, use plain milk. Coconut milk, however, enhances the flavour.

BURMESE FISH CURRY

2-2½ kg. fish – hilsa(shad) or any other bony fish

2 cups vinegar or more

3-4 fresh green or dry red chillis (optional)

2 tblsp. ginger paste

Water

3 tsp. salt or pepper to taste

3 tsp. turmeric

1½ cup mustard oil

4-5 tblsp. onion paste

5-6 tblsp. garlic paste

Method

Clean and wash fish. If one large fish is being used cut in large serving pieces. Rub with salt and turmeric and keep side for ½ hr. (In the case of small or medium fish, it can be left whole). Now soak in vinegar overnight. Make sure the fish pieces are covered by the vinegar.

Heat oil. If using dry red chillis add them now. When they start to splutter add all the ground spices. Fry for about 5 mins. Add the green chillis now if used. Add the fish and water just enough to cover. When water starts to boil cover pan and cook till all the bones are dissolved. From time to time uncover and stir. If a more yellow colour is required add a little more turmeric with the spices. At the end of it all there should be just enough gravy to cover the fish. Serve with rice.

STEAMED FISH BURMESE STYLE

500. gm. fish (with less bones) minced

2 tblsp. coconut paste

250 gm. onion chopped

1 tblsp. garlic chopped

2 tblsp. tender lemon grass chopped

1 green chilli deseeded and minced (optional)

10-12 cabbage leaves

Method

Put all the ingredients except cabbage leaves with salt and pepper to taste in the food-processor till smooth and well mixed. Trim cabbage leaves and soak in boiling hot water for 1 minute to make them easier to handle. Put filling in each cabbage leaf and roll like a sausage. Tie with thread or secure with toothpick. Put in a steamer for 10-15 minutes.

Variations:
1. Chicken or lamb mince may be prepared in the same way as above.
2. Instead of steaming the cabbage rolls, they may be shallow fried in oil after dipping them in beaten egg or a combination of flour and egg paste and lightly rolling them in bed crumbs, or, just rolling them in dry flour and frying them.
3. Fish ball curry – shape the fish in small balls (as in *koftas*) after going through the above processes. Omit the cabbage leaves. Use any fish curry recipe to make a curry sauce. When the sauce comes to the boil and the raw smell of spices disappear, drop the ball in carefully till done.
4. Prawn, chicken or lamb ball curry – may also be made as the fish ball curry.
5. If desired any of the ball or kofta curries may be fried in oil first and then dropped into the curry sauce. Use 1 tblsp flour or chickpea flour (*besan*) to prevent the koftas from disintegrating.

FISH SAS (PARSI FISH CURRY)

1 large onion chopped

¼ tsp. garlic paste

¼ tsp. mustard powder or, seeds

½ tsp. red chilli powder/paprika or to taste

2 green chillis (optional)

1 tsp. gram flour (*besan*)

500 gm. fish cut in serving pieces or, headless shrimps

Salt to taste

1 tsp. sugar.

¼ tsp. ginger paste

¼ tsp. turmeric powder

¼ tsp. cumin seeds

1 medium tomato chopped

1 cup water

1 tblsp. oil

1 egg

2 tblsp. vinegar

Method

Blend all the ingredients except *besan*, oil, egg, sugar, salt, and vinegar, together to a fine paste with 2 tblsp. of water. Heat oil and fry the paste well. Add the *besan* and let it mix well with the paste stirring continuously. Next add the water. Stir to mix and then add the fish/shrimps carefully. When cooked remove from heat and keep aside. Before serving mix the egg, sugar, and vinegar in a bowl. Heat the fish if it turns cold and pour the sauce over it. Remove from heat immediately and serve either with Parsi brown rice/*khitchri* or just plain steamed rice.

KHORISA (ASSAMESE BAMBOO PICKLE) and FISH CURRY

500 gm. fish cut in serving pieces

Salt to taste

4 tsp. ground onion

1-2 tblsp. (or more) *khorisa* **

2-3 fresh green chillis

2 tsp. turmeric powder

4-6 tblsp. mustard oil

2 tsp. each ground ginger and garlic

1 cup water

** see under "Miscellaneous" in this book set

Method

Smear the fish pieces with 1 tsp turmeric powder and salt. Keep aside for 5-10 mins. Heat oil to smoking and fry the fish a golden brown. Drain fish on paper towels. In the same oil fry well, the onion, garlic, ginger, and 1 tsp turmeric. Add the khorisa and cook for a few more minutes. Add water and salt and let it come to the boil. Add the green chillis and fish gently. Lower the heat, cover, and cook till the gravy penetrates the fish. Serve with plain boiled rice. If desired, add 2-3 chopped tomatoes with the spices while frying.

CHILLI FISH A LA BENGAL (I)

(This simple everyday fare of Bengal with each housewife having her own special touch.)

500 gm. fish – rub with salt and turmeric	6-8 tblsp. mustard oil
2 medium onions liquidized	1 tsp. turmeric paste
1 cup water	Salt to taste
3-4 green chillis – split but kept whole and seeds taken out	Coriander leaves as required for garnish

Method

Fry the fish in oil and keep aside. Leave 1 tblsp. of oil in pan and fry onion and

turmeric paste. Add water, salt to taste. Stir and let boil for 2-3 minutes till smell of raw spices disappears. Add the fish and green chilies. Cover and cook for another 2-3 minutes till gravy penetrates the fish. Be careful, fish does not break. The gravy should be just enough to cover the fish. Serve sprinkled with coriander leaves (optional) and plain rice.

Variation:

Can add 1 tsp. ginger liquidized or ground to the onion. turmeric paste.

CHILLI FISH A LA BENGAL (II)

4 tblsp. oil

3 tsp. mustard paste from rape seeds

4-6 or more green chillis

500 gm. fish – rub with turmeric, salt and fry as the previous recipe

½ tsp. whole mustard seeds

1 tsp. turmeric paste

½ cup water

Salt to taste

Method

In 1 tbsp. warm oil put in the whole mustard seeds. When they start popping, add the pastes, salt, green chillis and water. When it comes to the boil, add the fish. Cook another 4-5 minutes. Serve a in the previous recipe.

Variation:

Substitute mustard seeds with black cumin seeds.

BENGALI CHILLI FISH (III)

275 gm. (about 8 serving pieces) fish

Salt to taste

6-8 *boris* – dried lentil balls

1 tsp. each coriander and cumin powder

1 medium cauliflower cut into small florets

½-1 cup of water

2 green cardamoms split

2 tsp. turmeric powder

4 tblsp. oil

1 tsp. ginger paste

4-6 ripe red tomatoes chopped

4 medium potatoes cut in fours

2-3 fresh green chillis split

Method

Dust fish pieces with 1 tsp turmeric powder and a little salt. Rest for 5-10 minutes. Heat 2 tblsp. oil and fry the fish. Drain on paper towel and keep aside. Fry the boris, drain and keep aside. Add the rest of the oil to the pan and heat. Fry the ginger paste, coriander, cumin and the rest of the turmeric powder well, stirring frequently. Add the tomatoes and continue frying till well blended with the spices. Next add the cauliflower and potatoes. Fry all till well mixed with the spices. Add the water and cook till the vegetables are done. Now add the chillis, salt, *boris* and fish. Cook for another 5 minutes. Just before taking off the heat add the cardamom for extra flavour. Serve with plain steamed rice.

FISH JHAAL – CHILLI FISH (IV)

1 kg. fish cut in 16 serving pieces	Salt to taste
2-4 tsp. turmeric powder	½-¾ cup mustard oil
2 bay leaves	1-2 dry red chillis de-seeded
4 tblsp. ground onion	2 tblsp. ground ginger
1 tblsp. tomato soup powder	¼-½ tsp. Kashmiri chilli powder, *degi-mirch* or paprika
1 cup or more water	A pinch of '*ratanjote*' or red food colour
1-2 tblsp. fresh chopped coriander leaves	3-4 green chillis de-seeded

Method

Rub the fish pieces with the salt and a little turmeric powder. Leave aside till required. Pour enough oil to cover the base of a deep heavy bottomed or non-stick fry pan. Heat oil and fry the fish pieces slowly in lots without breaking. Remove fried fish and keep aside. Add 1-2 tblsp. oil only if necessary, in the same pan and heat. Add the bay leaves and red chillis. When they begin to splutter add all the rest of the ingredients combined in a bowl. Fry all well till brown sprinkling a little water if necessary. Add the water and let it come to the boil. Add salt to taste. Now lay the fried fish pieces gently in the gravy putting the green chillis on top. Cover and cook for a few minutes till the gravy penetrates the fish. The fish should not break. Sprinkle chopped coriander leaves on top before serving. Serve hot with steamed rice.

MA'S CABBAGE and FISH CURRY

500 gm. fish – bekti or similar variety	2-4 tblsp. oil
2-3 medium potatoes cubed small	1 large (approx. 1 kg.) cabbage shredded
2 tblsp. ground onion	2 tsp. ground ginger
2 tsp. ground garlic	1 tsp. cumin powder
1 tsp. turmeric powder	1 cup or less water
1 tblsp. ghee (butter oil or clarified butter)	½ tsp. garam masala powder

Method

Steam or pressure-cook fish. Take out all the bones and break up the fish. Heat oil and golden fry the cubed potatoes. Drain on paper towel and keep aside. Lightly fry the shredded cabbage. Add all the spices except the garam masala. When the spices are well mixed with the cabbage add the fish and the potatoes. Mix all well together. Now add the ghee and fry well adding water a little at a time so that the cabbage is cooked, and the spices do not stick to the pan. Continue cooking stirring frequently till all water disappears. This dish should be dry and well cooked. It requires a lot of frying. Just before taking off the heat, sprinkle garam masala powder on top. Serve with any Indian bread e.g. *chapattis* or simple *parathas*. It may also be served with lentils and rice.

Variation:

Shrimps or medium sized prawns may be used instead of fish. No need to boil shrimps or prawns before cooking. However, it is advisable to use headless, shelled, and de-veined shrimps or prawns.

COCONUT FISH

500 gm. any tasty fish cut in serving pieces

6-8 tblsp. mustard oil

1 tblsp ground ginger

1 cup thick coconut milk

1 bay leaf

2 cardamoms

1 medium onion thinly sliced

Salt to taste

2 tsp. turmeric powder

2 tblsp. ground onion

2 tsp. ground garlic

2-3 green chillis (optional)

½" piece cinnamon

2-3 cloves

1 tsp. paprika

Method

Rub fish pieces with 1 tsp. turmeric and salt. Heat half the oil, fry fish pieces and keep aside. Add 2 tblsp or more oil and heat. Add all the ground spices, 1 tsp turmeric powder and fry well. Add the coconut milk. When it comes to the boil add the fish pieces, salt and the green chillis. Cover and cook for 5 minutes or till the fish is well mixed with the spices and coconut milk. Take off heat. Now in another pan heat the rest of the oil (add a little more if necessary). Add the bay leaf, cinnamon, cardamom, cloves, onion slices and paprika in this order. Fry all till onions are a nice brown colour. Put the coconut fish back on heat and put all the fried ingredients with the oil into it. Take a bit of the coconut gravy and wash the pan where all the dry spices have been fried. Pour this on the fish. Cover and cook for a further 2-3 minutes before taking off the heat. Serve with rice.

YOGURT FISH

1 kg. fish cut in serving pieces (any kind that has less bones)

1 tsp. turmeric powder

4 tblsp. oil

1-2 bay leaves

2 medium onions sliced

2 medium onions ground

1" piece ginger ground

4 cups unsweetened yogurt well-beaten

1-2 fresh green chillis

¼ tsp. freshly roasted ground garam masala

Salt to taste

Method

Rub fish with a little turmeric and salt and let rest for a few minutes. Heat oil and lightly fry fish and keep aside. Pour more oil if necessary and heat. Add bay leaves and sliced onions. Fry lightly till onions change colour. Add the ground spices and fry a little more. Add the yogurt, green chillis, turmeric and salt. Let all come to the boil once. Add the fish and cook for a while till the fish blends well with the yogurt and the spices. Sprinkle with ¼ tsp. freshly roasted and ground garam masala. Serve with hot rice.

Variation:

Large or medium prawns, crayfish etc. can be used instead of fish.

GREEN CORIANDER FISH CURRY

1-2 bulbs or more garlic (according to the taste)	1 kg. or more fresh coriander leaves
1 tblsp. turmeric powder	If using fish – 1 kg. any large fish bekti, Rahu (carp), blue fish etc. cut in curry pieces
1-2 dry red chillis de-seeded (optional)	1 cup water
Salt to taste	2-4 tblsp. oil
3-4 whole fresh green chillis	4-5 whole fresh lemon leaves or, fresh lemon grass leaves.
2-4 tblsp. fresh lemon juice (optional)	

Method

Put the garlic and coriander leaves together with the water in a blender or food-processor to form a paste. If using fish -- rub fish with salt and turmeric and keep aside for 10-15 minutes. Heat oil and fry the fish pieces. Drain on paper towel. In the same oil add the dry red chilli if using. When it starts to splutter add the garlic coriander mixture. Stir to mix with oil. Now add turmeric, salt and the lemon or lemon grass leaves. Let the mixture cook till there is a thick gravy. Add the fish and green chillis. Make sure the gravy covers the whole. Cook some more till the gravy penetrates the flsh. Just before taking off heat add the lemon juice to taste and stir (i.e. if not using lemon or lemon grass leaves). If using any of the latter (which is preferable), gently take them out and discard after taking the curry off the heat. It should have a garlic- coriander- lemony flavour.

Variation:

Chicken can be cooked in the same way – 1.2 to 1.5 kg chicken cut in large curry pieces. Heat less oil, add the dry chilli and when it splutters add the chicken pieces. Fry till golden. Add the coriander mixture and all the rest of the ingredients proceeding as above. Add the green chillis when chicken is nearly ready. To cook chicken more water may be required. However, the gravy must be thick at the end of the cooking. 1-2 tblsp. ginger paste is often added with the garlic when cooking chicken. Personally, I prefer to leave it out.

Rice is a better accompaniment for the fish. The chicken may be served with either rice or any Indian bread

----

TOMATO FISH

(This is a recipe from my mother-in-law's repertoire. It is a very simple, tasty, easy dish which is also agreeable to the digestive system!)

500 gm. fish (preferably Rohu or any other rich big fish) cut in serving pieces	2 tsp. turmeric powder
4 tblsp. oil (preferably mustard oil)	1 tsp. whole black cumin seed
250 gm. ripe red tomatoes peeled and roughly chopped	2-3 whole green chillis split and deseeded
½ cup water or a little more	Salt to taste

½ bunch fresh coriander leaves chopped

Method

Rub fish pieces with a little salt and turmeric. Rest for 10-15 minutes to absorb. Heat oil and fry the fish pieces and lay aside. Add a little more oil only if necessary and put in the black cumin seeds. When they begin to splutter add the chopped tomatoes, remaining turmeric powder, and salt if desired. Cook stirring from time to time till tomatoes are soft. Add water and let all come to boil. Simmer for 5 mins. Gradually add the fried fish, cover, and cook for another 5 minutes. Uncover. Add the green chillis and coriander leaves. Cook for 2-3 minutes. Take off heat and serve with boiled rice. This dish should have just enough gravy to cover the fish and a little over.

Variations:

Medium sized prawns or chicken pieces may be used instead of fish. In the case of chicken or prawn no need to fry first. They should be added after the tomatoes, turmeric, and salt. The chicken may need more water and then the gravy could be simmered down.

MASALA (SPICED) FISH

(This is my mother's recipe and has been an all-time favourite of her children, their families, and friends. No matter what, it is never as good as she cooked it. Every time she made it, there was just that teeny bit of very subtle difference. I've tried my best to work out the following recipe from the handwritten slip she handed to me! This whole dish should be cooked on low heat from the beginning to the end.)

3-4 tblsp. oil or ghee	3-4 small bay leaves
3-4 tblsp. onion liquidized	2-3 tsp. fresh ginger ground
2 tsp. fresh garlic ground	1-2 tsp. turmeric powder
½ tsp. tomato powder or, 1 tblsp tomato paste	1 kg. fish cut in serving pieces
2 tblsp. raisins whole or ground	2 tblsp. red vinegar
½ tsp. sugar	Salt to taste
1 tblsp. almond slivers	1-2 tblsp. carrots grated
1 cup water	

Method

Warm oil and add bay leaves. When they begin to splutter add the onion, ginger, garlic and turmeric, tomato paste, or powder mixed together in a bowl. Fry all well. Lay fish on the spices. When one side is done turn over and cook the other side till done. Add the water if necessary and cook till done. In a bowl mix the raisins, vinegar, sugar, and salt and pour over fish. Cook a few minutes longer. Most of the liquid should disappear and the fish should be in a thick gravy. Serve on a flat dish and garnish with almonds and carrot. Serve with a simple pilau or plain steamed rice.

Variations:
1. This dish is best cooked with a whole fish and is more a party fare.
2. 1-2 cups thick coconut milk can be used instead of plain water. In this case omit the tomato paste or powder.

SORSÉ (MUSTARD) FISH

4-6 tblsp. oil (preferably mustard oil)

½ tsp. whole black mustard seeds

1 tblsp. onion paste

Salt to taste

2-3 whole green chillis

500 gm. fish cut in serving pieces

2-3 tblsp. '*sorse*' (mustard/rye) paste

2 tsp. ginger paste

1 tsp. turmeric powder

Method

Heat oil. Fry fish pieces lightly after smearing with a little salt and turmeric. Drain and keep aside. Pour off excess oil if any leaving about 1 tblsp. Add the mustard seeds. When they begin to splutter add the sorsé, onion and ginger pastes already combined in a bowl. At this time also add the salt, turmeric and green chillis. Mix all well and let come to a boil. Place the fish carefully in the pan. Cook a further few minutes to let the juices penetrate the fish. Take off heat and serve with plain boiled rice. When the fish is done there should be very little thick gravy. Add very little water only if necessary, during cooking.

HILSA (SHAD) WITH MUSTARD, COCONUT AND POPPYSEED

1-1½ kg. *hilsa** cut in serving pieces

2 tsp. turmeric powder

1-2 bay leaves

1 whole dry chilli de-seeded

1-2 tblsp. white poppy seed (*posto*) paste

Water as required

Salt to taste

3-4 tblsp. oil

½ tsp. black cumin seeds

2-4 tblsp. mustard (*sorsé*) paste

2-4 tblsp. coconut paste

2-3 fresh green chillis de-seeded

* Shad

Method

Rub fish pieces with a little salt and turmeric. Heat oil. Add bay leaves, black cumin seeds and the red chilli. When the seeds start spluttering add all the pastes and fry stirring continuously till a nice aroma of *posto* emanates. Add turmeric, water, and salt to taste. When it comes to the boil, place the fish gently in the pan. Place the green chillis on the fish. Cover and simmer till fish is done. Serve with plain white rice.

FISH JHOLE

250 gm. fish in curry pieces

2 tsp. turmeric powder

2 medium potatoes quartered

½ tsp. black cumin seeds

1 tsp. each coriander and cumin powder

1-1½ cups water

Salt to taste

2 tblsp. oil (preferably mustard oil)

2 medium carrots halved and cut lengthwise

1-2 medium tomatoes chopped

2 green chillis

1 tblsp. fresh coriander leaves chopped

Method

Rub the fish pieces with a little salt and 1 tsp. turmeric powder. Rest for 15 minutes to harden the fish so that, it does not break during cooking. Heat oil and fry the fish pieces 2-3 at a time. Keep aside. In the same oil, sauté the potatoes and then the carrots and set aside. Again, in the same pan add 1 tsp. more of oil, if necessary. Add the black cumin seeds. When they begin to splutter add the sautéed vegetables and tomatoes. Cook and stir from time to time for about 5 minutes. Mix the coriander, cumin, and the rest of the turmeric powder in the water and pour over the vegetables. Cover and cook till vegetables are done. Add the fish, salt and the chillis. Cook for another 5 minutes or till the gravy penetrates the fish. Sprinkle coriander leaves before removing from heat. Serve with rice and lime quarters if you like.

Variation:

1. Carrots may be substituted with a small cauliflower separated into florets or, 1-2 green bananas peeled, halved and cut lengthwise or in thick rounds or 4-5 *patals* (palwal) cut in twos or threes depending on the size. A handful of green peas may also be added with any of the vegetables.

2. 6-8 *boris* (dried balls of different lentil pastes – available in any Indian grocery/provision store. The Bengali boris are milder than the North Indian boris) fried and added during the last few minutes of cooking add to the flavour of the *jhole*. The boris can be added whole or broken, after frying.

3. Alternately, do not sauté the vegetables being used. Instead, boil them covered with the water and spice powders till done. The tomatoes may or may not be cooked with the vegetables. Add the fried fish, chillis and salt and cook as above. Heat 1-2 tsp. oil (preferably mustard oil). Add the black cumin seeds. When they begin to splutter add the tomatoes (if not already cooked with the vegetables) for 2-3 minutes. Pour over the jhole and let all come to boil once more. Add the coriander leaves as above, remove from heat, and serve.

CHANCHRA OR BENGALI DRY VEGETABLE AND FISH HEAD CURRY

1 fish head and bones of carp (*rohu*) or shad (*hilsa*)	1 tsp. turmeric powder
300 gm. red pumpkin cut into cubes	2 medium potatoes each cut into eight pieces
2-4 tblsp. oil	Salt to taste
4-6 broad beans cut in half	1 large eggplant cut into cubes
1-2 sweet potatoes cut in cubes	1 large radish cut in cubes
1-2 fresh green chillis split and deseeded	2 small onions minced
½ tsp. *panchphoron*	1 dry red chilli

Method

Chop the fish head and bones roughly and mix with a little salt and turmeric powder. Keep aside to rest for a few minutes. Heat 2 tblsp. oil and lightly fry the head and bones. Keep aside. Add a little more oil, if necessary, heat and then add all the vegetables and keep frying till half done. Add the rest of the turmeric powder, salt to taste and the green chillis. Keep frying a little longer till done sprinkling a little water from time to time so that the curry does not stick to the bottom of the pan. No extra water besides this is required. When the vegetables are almost cooked add the fish head and bones and keep cooking stirring from time to time till all well fried and mushy. Take off heat and keep aside. Heat 1-2 tsp. oil. Add the onion, *panchphoron* and red chilli. When the seeds begin to splutter add the vegetable curry, stir well to mix, and then remove from heat. Serve with rice and lentils (*dal*).

MALAYSIAN LOBSTER or PRAWN CURRY (LOBSTER RENDANG)

(This dish is best with lobsters or Cray fish. However, in their absence, large prawns may be substituted. Definitely not a dish to be made with small prawns or shrimps.)

500 gm. lobster or Cray fish or large prawns).

Sauce:

1 large or, 2 small coconuts

Water as required

4 tblsp. oil

1" fresh ginger minced or ground

½ tsp. turmeric powder

2 fresh green chillis

Juice of 2 limes

3 large onions thinly sliced

6 fat cloves of garlic crushed

2 bouillon cubes

Salt to taste

Method

Broil shelled fish after brushing with oil either on charcoal or under the grill. After broiling, cut the lobster or Cray fish into large serving chunks. In case of prawns, keep whole or cut in half. Remove shells, tail, and heads.

Grate coconut. Add enough water to just soak but not drown it. Let stand 15-30 minutes. Squeeze well to take out thick milk about 1 cup. Keep aside. Soak in water once again and repeat the above process. This is the thin milk. Keep aside. Warm oil, fry onions, ginger, garlic, turmeric, well, sprinkling with the thin coconut milk from time to time. Do not let spices burn. Stir continuously. When spices exude a favourable aroma, add the 2 bouillon cubes diluted in the rest of the thin milk. Let come to boil. Lower heat. Add shellfish and thick coconut milk. Cover and simmer 10-15 minutes. Add chilies, salt, and lime juice. Cook another 2-3 minutes and take off fire. serve with boiled rice. This dish is best cooked just before eating to enjoy the fresh flavours.

Note:

Instead of using fresh coconut canned or packet coconut milk, cream or powder can be used. Add water to get thin and thick milk according to instructions or from own judgment.

LAU (WHITE GOURD) WITH SHRIMPS

This is a popular dish of Bengal, and every household has its own little touch which makes the taste differ from house to house. This is just a simple basic recipe. You may also add your own little bit to give it that special flavour.

1 kg. white gourd grated and steamed	Salt to taste
2 tblsp. oil	1-2 tbsp. water
250 gm. headless small shrimps cleaned	2-4 whole green chillis – de-seeded
1 tsp. coriander powder	A pinch of sugar or, gourmet powder
1 tsp. cumin powder	Coriander leaves for garnish
½ tsp. or more, turmeric powder	

Method

Heat 1 tblsp. oil. Sauté the shrimps and keep aside. In the same pan, warm another 1 tblsp. oil. Fry well a paste of coriander, cumin, turmeric, and salt to taste with 1-2 tblsp. of water. Add the gourd and shrimps and fry with spices till well coated. Add water only if necessary. (The end product should be dry but mushy). Cover and cook to dry water. Add 2-4 green chilies for flavour and, a pinch of sugar or gourmet powder. Serve sprinkled with coriander leaves.

Variations:

1. In the absence of shrimps, use any other fish with less bones. Frying breaking up the fish. In small chunks before cooking with the spices.
2. Instead of fish, use 125 gm. good spicy Bengal "Boris". Fry and keep them aside. Add them to the gourd at the last minute of cooking and cook 5 more minutes after mixing and slightly breaking them up.

SHRIMP AND CAULIFLOWER

1 tblsp. oil

125 gm. cauliflower cut into small florets

125 gm. shrimps with or without heads

1 tblsp. spring onions chopped

1 tsp. black or white mustard paste

Salt to taste

1-1½ tblsp. grated coconut (optional)

1 bay leaf

2 medium potatoes cut in eighths

1 large onion sliced thickly

1 small capsicum chopped fine

½ tsp. turmeric paste

½-¾ cup warm water

1-2 fresh green chillis whole

Method

Heat oil and add the bay leaf. When it starts to sizzle add the cauliflower and potatoes to brown slightly. Next add the shrimps, onion, spring onions and capsicum. Stir fry for a couple of minutes. Mix the mustard, turmeric and salt in the water and then pour over the shrimps. Let all come to a boil, lower heat, cover and cook till vegetables are done. Add the coconut and green chillis, stir, cook for another 2-3 minutes. Three quarters of the liquid should dry up once the vegetables are done. This dish should not be mushy. Increase or decrease the water as required. If there is too much water, uncover to dry off some of the liquid. Serve with rice or any Indian bread.

MUMMY'S PUMPKIN and PRAWN CURRY

4 tblsp. oil	2-3 medium potatoes quartered
1 bay leaf	3-4 cloves garlic
1 large onion ground to paste	1 tsp. turmeric powder
500 gm. red pumpkin cubed	½ cup water
250. gm. headless prawns or shrimps	2-3 fresh green chillis (optional)
Salt to taste	2 tblsp. coriander leaves chopped for garnish

Method

Heat oil and lightly fry the potatoes till golden. Keep aside. Add bay leaf and stir for 1 minute. Next add the garlic. When it begins to brown add the onion paste and turmeric. Fry for a few minutes sprinkling a little water at a time. Now add the pumpkin and then the potatoes. Mix with the spices and keep frying till there is a nice aroma. Sprinkle water a little at a time so that the spices and vegetables do not stick to the bottom and sides of the pan. Add enough water, if necessary, to cook the vegetables, cover and simmer till almost done. Some water will come out from the pumpkin, which may help to cook the vegetables without any extra water. Add the shrimps, chillis broken in half and salt to taste. Cook a little more till all done and most of the water disappears. The curry should be mushy when ready without the vegetables and shrimps breaking. Sprinkle chopped coriander leaves before serving. Good eating with rice or any Indian bread.

PRAWNS IN DAAB (GREEN COCONUT)

500 gm. medium sized prawns   1 young green coconut – cut the top and pour out the water

Method

Marinate the prawns in your favourite spices and plenty of oil. Fill coconut with prawn mixture and a little of the coconut water (The amount of water and oil will depend on the recipe). Put back the top and seal well with a glue of flour and water. Cook in a medium hot oven for about 10-15 minutes. Prawns do not take very long to cook. You can either serve it in the coconut with the top removed once again, OR, turn out into a dish with some of the coconut scrapings from the sides. Serve with rice.

A few suggestions for the prawn marinade —

1. This is the most popular among many - Make a paste of mustard and turmeric (2-3 tbsp. mustard, 1-2 tbsp. turmeric, 3-4 tbsp. mustard oil, salt, 3-4 green chilies whole). Mix all these with the prawns. You can mix ½ tsp. black cumin seed with the marinade. Alternatively, warm 2 tsp. mustard oil. Put in ½ tsp. black cumin seeds. When seeds start spluttering, add to the marinade.

2. Make a marinade of 1-2 large ground onion, 2-3 tsp. ground ginger, 1-2 tsp. ground garlic, 1 bay leaf, 3-4 tsp. beaten yoghurt, salt to taste, green chilies (optional), 3-4 tbsp. vegetable or mustard oil, 1 tbsp. tomato puree. When prawns are ready, gently stir in ½ tsp. 'garam masala' powder. Alternatively, add ½" stick of cinnamon, 2-3 small cardamoms, 1-2 whole cloves. Omit the addition of garam masala powder at the end.

3. Use any of the prawn recipes given in the book as a marinade. You can do the initial frying of the spices and prawns on top of the stove and then fill the green coconut. In this case, the cooking time will be less. OR, just fry the spices, take off fire, mix in the prawns. Fill.

For the liquid, always use the coconut water instead plain water.

Have fun!

PRAWN CURRY (I)

4 tblsp. oil

1-2 large onions chopped

2 tsp. cumin powder

1 tblsp. fresh ginger paste

¼ tsp. sugar

4 tblsp. unsweetened yogurt

1 cup coconut milk extract

1 bay leaf

4-6 cloves garlic chopped

2 tsp. coriander powder

1½ tsp. turmeric powder

Salt to taste

8 large prawns, (preferably Cray fish)

Method

Heat oil. Add bay leaf and then onion, garlic, and fry till golden brown. Add rest of spices, sugar, and salt. Fry well, adding the yoghurt a little at a time so that the spices do not stick to pan. Add prawns and fry with spices on low heat. Add remainder of the yoghurt while frying. When prawns are well mixed with the spices, add the coconut milk. Cook till prawns are done. Add a little more of thick coconut extract, if needed. Cook till prawns are done. Gravy should be thick. Sprinkle with 'garam masala' powder before taking off heat.

PRAWN CURRY (II)

1 kg. prawns without heads	1 tsp. red chilli powder (optional)
½ tsp. turmeric powder	¼ tsp. black ground pepper

Sauce:

½ medium coconut grated	2 green seeded chillis finely minced (optional)
3 medium onions ground	Curry leaves
3 cups yogurt	

Tempering:

1 tblsp. oil	¼ tsp. whole mustard seeds
½ tsp. whole cumin seeds	3 finely minced onions

Method

Rub the prawns with the spices. Mix well. Add sufficient water. Cook till prawns are done.

Mix the sauce ingredients and beat well. Cook on high heat till it comes to boil. Add 3 sprigs curry leaves. Remove after 2 minutes. Add cooked prawns to sauce.

Heat oil in a small pan. Add cumin, mustard seeds, and onion. When they start sputtering and onion is browning, pour over prawns and stir. Serve with rice or any Indian bread.

PRAWNS IN COCONUT SAUCE (I)

1 kg. medium sized prawns

2 tsp. fresh ginger paste

4 medium onions sliced

Whole green chillis with seeds taken out – according to the taste 3-4 more or less

Salt to taste

1 tsp. turmeric

1 tsp. powdered fenugreek (*Methi*)

5-6 curry leaves

1 large coconut or 2 mediums (extract 2 lots of milk—first thick and then about 2 cups thin.)

1 tblsp. fresh lime juice

Method

Put all the ingredients including prawns in a saucepan and bring to boil. Lower heat and simmer till prawns are done. Pour in the thick coconut milk — about 1 cup. Simmer 5 minutes. Add lime juice. Take off fire and serve with rice.

FISH or PRAWNS IN COCONUT SAUCE (II)

(This recipe can be made with fish or prawns)

2 tblsp. oil	2 medium onions sliced
½ tsp. fresh ginger paste	4-5 curry leaves
2 medium sliced onions	1-2 slit green chillis (optional)
1 tblsp. vinegar or less	1 medium to large coconut – extract ½ cup thick and 1 cup thin milk.
Salt to taste	500 gm. fish – keep whole or fillet without cutting in slices

Method

Heat oil. Sauté onions. When it gets opaque, add all other ingredients except fish. Add thin coconut milk. Bring it to boil. Add fish. Lower heat and simmer till fish is done. Add vinegar, stir. Remove from heat and serve with rice.

Variation:

For both the above recipes, you can fry the fish lightly before adding the ingredients. No need to fry prawns before cooking. Rub salt and turmeric before frying fish.

PRAWN CURRY IN COCONUT SAUCE (III)

2 large onions finely sliced	Salt to taste
1-2 split seeded green chillis (optional)	1 tsp cumin powder
1 tsp. turmeric	½ tsp. red chilli powder (optional)
1½ cup thick milk of 1 coconut	2 tsp. garlic paste
500 gm. medium sized prawns	Juice of 1 lime or, 1 tblsp. tamarind juice

Method

In sauce pan lay onions, sprinkle with salt and green chillis. Mix all thoroughly pressing with the back of a wooden spoon. Add all the spices and coconut milk. When it starts boiling add prawns, lower heat, and simmer till ready. Add lime or tamarind juice before taking off fire. Serve with rice.

This dish can be made both with chicken or fish. Prawn cooked this way requires no oil.

QUICK PRAWN MALAI (COCONUT MILK) CURRY (IV)

2 tblsp. oil	1-2 bay leaves
2 large onions sliced	800 gm. medium prawns with heads
4 tblsp. spring onions chopped	½ pt. thick coconut milk
1 tsp. turmeric powder	Salt to taste
2-3 fresh whole green chillis	1-2 tblsp. grated coconut
1 tsp garam masala powder freshly roasted	1-2 tblsp. fresh coriander leaves for garnish

Method

Warm the oil. Add the bay leaves, onion, and the prawns all together in this order. When the onions become transparent and the prawns turn red add the spring onions and stir. Next add the coconut milk, turmeric powder, salt to taste and the chillis. Cook for a few minutes longer till all well mixed and the prawns are done. Now add the grated coconut, stir and cook for 2-3 minutes. Sprinkle garam masala powder. Remove from heat and garnish with chopped coriander leaves. This curry should have very little gravy. Serve with rice or any Indian bread.

PRAWN MALAD

2-3 tblsp. oil

2-3 tblsp. grated coconut

A pinch of sugar

3 large onions sliced

Salt to taste

1 cup water

1 tblsp. ground mustard paste or, powder

3 seeded and slit green chillis (optional)

1 tblsp. tomato purée

2 tsp. turmeric powder

500 gm. medium to large sized prawns

Few coriander leaves

Method

Heat oil. Add mustard, coconut, sugar, chillis, tomato purée, sliced onion, turmeric, and salt. Cook slowly on low heat. Add prawns when a pleasant aroma of fried spices emanates. Add water and cook till fish is done and there is a thick gravy. Garnish with coriander leaves.

PRAWNS AND TOMATO

4 tblsp. mustard or peanut oil

2 tsp. garlic paste

1 tsp. turmeric powder

500 gm. medium sized prawns cleaned with heads and tails left on. (If heads are not liked, cut them off and cook with enough water in a saucepan for 15 minutes or, in the pressure cooker for 5 minutes till done. Cool and strain the liquid. Put it aside for use in the curry – this gives the red colour. Throw away the rest of the scum.

¼ bunch coriander leaves chopped

2 tblsp. onion paste

3-4 large tomatoes quartered

2-3 green chillis deseeded

2 tsp. "Fish and Fish" sauce or any other fish sauce, 'balachong' (pickled prawn) or fish paste

1-1½ cup water or liquid from prawn heads.

Method

Heat oil. Add onion, garlic, turmeric, and fish paste. Fry all well. Now add the prawns, tomatoes, chillis and coriander leaves. Fry all together for about 2 mins till all well mixed. Add the water or prawn liquid and salt to taste. Cover and cook till prawns are done and there is a thick gravy. Serve hot with plain boiled rice.

Variations:

Use any rich fish with less bones instead of prawns. Fry the fish first after rubbing with turmeric and salt. Salt should be used judiciously as the fish pastes are usually salty.

(STEAMED) MUSTARD PRAWNS OR FISH

(Again, a very popular Bengali dish which has different variations. This is usually served with rice.)

250 gm. prawns (with or without heads) or, whitefish or, fillets or, cuts in serving pieces

-3 tsp. turmeric powder

2 tblsp. mustard oil

2-3 tsp. mustard powder

Salt to taste

2-3 green chillis

Water as required

Method

Grease the bottom and sides of an oven-proof dish. Rub prawns or fish well with salt and turmeric and place in the dish evenly. Make a thick paste with the mustard, turmeric, salt, and water. Cover fish with this paste packing sides and gaps between the fish well. Place green chilies on top. Pour. mustard oil evenly on top. Cover dish and place in a steamer or, in a saucepan of water. Make sure no water goes into the dish. Cooking time is around 20-25 minutes depending on the thickness and size of prawns or fish.

Alternatively, this can be cooked in a medium hot oven for 5-10 minutes or, in the microwave power 7 for 2-4 minutes.

Variations

1. Omit the oil. Increase water a very little.
2. In the original recipe, sprinkle ½ tsp. black cumin seed.
3. Paturi — Line dish with one big banana leaf which should hang over the sides. Continue as the main recipe using black cumin seeds (optional) and place on banana leaves. Pull up the banana leaves from the sides and wrap well like a parcel. Secure the opening well so that no juice escapes from the fish. Cover and put this in a moderately hot oven and cook till done — 15-20 minutes. It can be served on the banana leaf by placing the parcel on the serving dish and opening the leaf.
4. Proceed as per "Paturi" instructions. Instead of cooking in the oven, place parcel on a hot griddle (tawa) on top of the stove. When the leaf starts wrinkling, carefully turn parcel with two spatulas. Cook till ready.

In this case, to serve, the contents have to be put on another dish as the leaves get disfigured. However, the prawns/fish absorb the banana leaf juices and the dish exudes an aroma to satisfy the palate!

PRAWNS OR FISH IN THE OVEN

250 gm. Prawns or fish slices

3 tblsp. mustard or vegetable oil

1 dry red chilli

¼ cup water

¼ tsp. turmeric powder 9optional) for colour

1 bunch coriander leaves

2 tsp. turmeric powder for rubbing

½ tsp. whole black mustard seed

1 tsp. ginger paste

4 tblsp. mustard paste

1-2 green chillis

Salt to taste

Method

Rub fish with turmeric and salt. Keep aside ½ hour. In 2 tblsp. oil fry fish, keep aside. Add rest of oil, if necessary, to pan. Put in whole mustard seed and red chilli. When it splutters add ginger paste and fry a little. Add the water. Let come to boil. Lower heat and simmer 5 minutes. Pour spiced liquid in an oven-proof dish. Add salt and mix. Add a little more water to the mustard paste if necessary. Strain into dish. Add turmeric if desired. Put prawns or fish into the dish. See that the fish is immersed in the sauce. Lay whole green chilies on top of fish. Cover and put in a medium hot oven and cook 5-10 minutes. When almost done, sprinkle coriander leaves over fish and cook a few more minutes in the oven. Serve with rice and a salad. There should be enough water in the dish for fish to be cooked. When ready, it should have a thick gravy.

Variation

Follow the same procedure as above. Instead of cooking in the oven, put in the microwave power 7 for 5 minutes, which should complete cooking time. Cook for another 2-3 minutes after adding coriander leaves.

SHRIMP or FISH IN BANANA LEAVES (FISH PĀTURI)

8 or more banana leaves

500 gm. fresh headless shrimps or fish cut in serving pieces or whole

4-6 tblsp. oil preferably mustard oil

1 tsp turmeric powder (optional)

3-4 tsp. white mustard ground

Salt to taste

2-3 green chillis or more

Method

Wash banana leaves, dry, and rub with oil. Lay half the amount of leaves on top of each other lengthwise. Next lay the rest of the leaves on top of each other across the first half. Coat the shrimps/fish with salt, mustard and turmeric powder and a generous amount of oil. Arrange on the banana leaves side by side carefully (do not place in a heap). Put the green chillis on top. Cover by folding over the leaves from the sides like a parcel. Tie with a string if necessary. Place parcel on a griddle and cover whole with a deep curved lid or another pan. Cook on medium heat. When the lower side of the parcel gets burnt, turn over carefully and cook the other side similarly. Before serving, open parcel and lift contents carefully on to a serving dish. Serve with plain boiled rice.

Alternately fish paturi can be cooked in the oven or microwave. The taste is much better cooked on top of the stove on a griddle. Instead of banana leaves aluminium foil can also be used in which case do not microwave. Foil is less messy but then again banana leaves bring out the flavour of the dish. To microwave follow the same method but instead of banana leaves/foil place fish in a microwave safe dish with cover.

Use commercially packed mustard powder made into a paste with a little water or grind white or black mustard seeds with a little salt and 1 green chilli and rest for 1 hour to take away the bitter taste of the mustard.

SIMPLE LIGHT PRAWN KOFTA CURRY

250 gm. medium prawns or shrimps

2-3 fresh green chillis (optional)

1 tblsp. oil

1 tblsp. onion paste

1 tsp. ginger paste

1 tsp. cumin powder

¼ cup chopped tomatoes or, 2-4 tblsp. unsweetened yogurt

2 tblsp. fresh coriander leaves for garnish

Salt to taste

1 tblsp. flour, corn flour or *besan*

2-3 bay leaves

½ tsp. garlic paste (optional)

1 tsp. coriander powder

1 tsp. turmeric powder

½ tsp. freshly roasted garam masala powder

1-1½ cup warm water or, as required

Method

Put the prawns cleaned and without heads in the food processor or through a mincer. Add salt, 1 green chilli de-seeded and minced fine and corn flour or substitute to bind. (If using *besan* dry roast first till there is a nice aroma). Dust palms with dry flour and form small balls or *koftas* with the prawn mixture. Keep aside.

Heat the oil in a deep pan. Add the bay leaves. When they begin to splutter add all the spices except *garam masala* powder. Keep stirring and frying the spices. When they begin to stick to the bottom of the pan add the tomatoes or yogurt and continue frying stirring frequently and scraping the bottom. When there is no raw spice smell and there is a fine curry aroma add warm water and bring to the boil. Add the prawn balls, whole remaining green chillis and salt. Lower heat and simmer till done and there is a fairly medium thick gravy. Take off heat and sprinkle garam masala powder. Garnish with chopped coriander leaves. Serve with rice.

Variation:

If preferred the prawn balls may be rolled in dry flour and then shallow fried. Drain on paper towel and place in a deep dish. Make the curry sauce as above adding the water after the spices are done. Simmer stirring from time to time till ready. Pour over the fried prawn balls. Sprinkle garam masala powder and garnish with coriander leaves as above.

Alternately drop the fried koftas into the curry sauce. Simmer for a few minutes to let the sauce penetrate inside the koftas.

CRAB CURRY

(Most people cook crab in the curry form with the shell on. This necessitates using one's fingers. I dislike using my fingers to eat to eat even the simplest items such as drumsticks. There are several reasons why I prefer using cutlery to eat whenever possible because (1) I can never get my fingers to accurately deliver food to my mouth. (2) The smell of food remains on my fingers for hours, no matter how well I wash, perfume, and cream my hands. (3) Finally, I find the whole business very messy and nauseating. So, I derived my own method of making crab curry, which can be eaten with ease.)

4 large to medium sized crabs — scalded or put under the grill till shells turn red. Scalding is better in boiling water. Pull the shell off. Discard stomach bag attached to shell below the eyes — it is greenish in colour. Also discard the greyish white dead man's fingers. Cut each crab into 4 pieces. Gently lift the meat out of the shell — try to keep them as whole in chunks as possible. You will, however, get some shredded meat which may also be used. Crack the claws and extract the meat from them also.

Another alternative is to buy frozen raw crab meat in packets from the supermarkets.

2 tblsp. oil	1 bay leaf
1 pc. ½" cinnamon stick	1 tblsp. onion paste
2 tsp. garlic paste	2 tsp. fresh ginger paste
¼ tsp. cumin powder	2 tsp. coriander powder
¼ tsp turmeric powder	4-5 red chopped ripe tomato
1 cup thick coco nut milk	Salt to taste
Fresh coriander leaves for garnish	

Method

Heat oil. Add bay leaf and cinnamon. Next add all the ground spices and fry well. Add the crab meat and mix well. Let the spices incorporate into the crab. Add coconut milk, chopped tomatoes and salt. Cover and cook till done and no smell of raw spices remain. Sprinkle with chopped coriander leaves before serving.

Variation:

Instead of coconut milk, use 1 cup beaten, unsweetened yogurt. Discard cinnamon stick — use only the bay leaf. Fry the chopped tomatoes with the spices. Add the yoghurt with the crab and fry well. Sprinkle with garam masala powder before serving. Green chillis can be added whole at the last minute of cooking.

CRAB KOFTA CURRY

4 crabs – prepared as the previous recipe with the meat minced

4 tblsp. oil

1 bay leaf

1 tsp. ground garlic paste

1 tsp. turmeric powder

2-3 tblsp. yogurt

Salt to taste

¼ tsp. garam masala powder

2 egg whites

2 tblsp. corn flour

1 dry red chilli

2 large onions sliced

2 tsp. ground ginger paste

1 tblsp. tomato purée

1 cup hot water

3-4 whole green chillis (optional)

1 tblsp. chopped coriander leaves

Method

Mix crab mince, beaten egg white and corn flour well. Make into small balls. Fry in oil till golden brown. Drain and keep aside. Add a little more oil to pan only if necessary. Put in the dry chilli and bay leaf. After ½ minute add the onions and fry till transparent and turning lightly golden. Now add all the spices including tomato puree. Fry spices well adding yogurt from time to time till all used up and, there is a nice aroma of spices. Add 1 cup hot water and let all come to boil. Add salt and put in the koftas and the green chillis, let cook covered for 5 minutes on low heat. Sprinkle garam masala powder and chopped coriander leaves before serving.

GOAN CHICKEN CURRY

1 tblsp. oil	4 tblsp. butter
2 large onions sliced	2 large tomatoes chopped
1 large (approx. 1½ kg. chicken cut into serving pieces)	4 tblsp. ground garlic paste
1 tsp. turmeric powder	4 tblsp. ground ginger paste
2 tblsp. tomato purée	4-6 fresh coriander leaves chopped
4-5 green chillis (optional)	Salt to taste
Warm water as required	

Method

Heat butter and oil. Fry sliced onions till brown. Add tomatoes and continue frying till soft. Now add chicken pieces and continue frying for about 10 minutes. Next add all the dry and wet spices, coriander leaves and tomato purée. Mix all well, cover and cook on slow fire till chicken is done and no raw smell of the spices linger. Add salt and green chillis before taking off fire. Add warm water a little at a time only if required. This should have a thickish gravy with the oil floating on top. Serve with rice or any Indian bread.

Variations:

The fresh coriander leaves may be ground into a paste with 1 whole bulb garlic and 2" piece ginger into a paste. Continue the rest of the cooking as above. May garnish with whole or chopped green chillis, coriander leaves and 1 or 2 medium tomatoes quartered and slightly softened during the last minute of cooking.

BENGALI CHICKEN CURRY

1 large chicken (1½ kg. approx.) cut in serving pieces

4 tblsp. oil

4 medium potatoes washed, scraped, and halved (optional)

2 large onions sliced thinly

1½-2 tsp. turmeric powder

1 tsp. sugar

½ cup warm water

½ tsp. powdered 'garam masala' (Bengali) dry roasted

1 cup yogurt well beaten

1 bay leaf

1 dry red chilli without seeds

2 tsp. each of coriander and cumin powder

1 tblsp. fresh ginger ground

Salt to taste

1-2 whole green chillis (optional)

Method

Marinate chicken in plain yogurt for 2-3 hours. Heat oil. Fry the potatoes (if using) golden brown. and then keep aside. Now put bay leaf and red dry chilli. When they start to splutter add the sliced onions and fry till golden. Now add all the spices, sugar, and salt. Fry well. Add the chicken with the yoghurt. Cook till colour of chicken changes to a light brown. Now add the potatoes and stir well to coat them with the spices. Add sufficient water to cook chicken and potatoes. Let come to boil, cover stirring from time to time till curry is ready. Can add whole green chillis during the last couple of minutes of cooking. Sprinkle with garam masala before taking off heat.

Variations:

1. Can omit the red chilli and use ½ tsp chilli powder with the spices.
2. At the beginning fry 1" cinnamon, 4 whole cloves, 3 whole green cardamoms or, 1 black large cardamom with the bay leaf. Omit the garam masala powder at the end. Instead, sprinkle 1 finely sliced onion fried crisp on the curry before serving.
3. Instead of using red chilli and chilli powder, substitute with fresh green chilli split and deseeded during the last few minutes of the cooking.

Either sprinkle with garam masala powder just before taking off heat or, garnish with crispy fried onion slices.

THICK CHICKEN CURRY

1 large chicken (approx. 1½ kg.) cut in serving pieces	½-1 cup yogurt
4 large tomatoes chopped	2-4 tblsp. oil
4 large onions chopped	4 green cardamoms
2 bay leaves	4 cloves
1" piece cinnamon	2 tblsp. each ginger and garlic paste
2 tblsp. onion paste	1 tblsp. turmeric powder
2 tblsp. powdered coriander and cumin	Fresh green chillis (optional)
Salt to taste	1 tblsp. crisply fried onions or, chopped coriander leaves for garnishing
Water as required for cooking	

Method

Marinate chicken in beaten yogurt. Cook the tomatoes and chopped onions together till mushy and well blended. Keep aside. Heat oil, add bay leaves, cardamoms, cinnamon, cloves. When they begin to splutter add all the rest of the spices in paste and powder form. Fry well till raw smell disappears and there is a nice aroma. Add the chicken with the yoghurt and fry some more till chicken pieces are well covered in the spices. Now add the tomatoes and onion mixture. Cook some more. Add salt and green chillis. Add water only if necessary. Cover and cook till chicken is done. This curry should be thick. Garnish according to your choice. Serve with pilau, plain boiled rice or any kind of Indian bread.

Variations:

1. Can add 2 red dry chillis at the beginning of cooking with the bay leaves etc. In this case omit the green chillis unless you have a preference for a hot curry.
2. The tomato and onion mixture may be added with the spices and fried all together.

3. If a more brownish curry is preferred omit the turmeric and tomatoes. Use double the quantity of chopped onions which should be cooked with a little water till soft and then mashed. Also use double the quantity of coriander powder. This recipe may also be used in making mutton, fish, paneer (cottage cheese) or a mixed vegetable curry. The fish curry is particularly delicious. Use Bekti or similar fish with not too many bones. No need to fry the fish first. In the case of paneer – cut it in cubes and lightly fry, or it may disintegrate.

CHICKEN CURRY (I)

4 tblsp. (or less) oil	2 medium onions sliced
4-5 cloves garlic	1½-2 kg. whole chicken cut into serving pieces
2 tsp. ground ginger	
1 tsp. heaped turmeric powder	1 tsp. black cumin seeds pounded
2-3 green chillis split and deseeded	1 bunch fresh coriander leaves chopped
1 cup yogurt	Salt to taste
½ tsp. sugar	Water as required

Method

Heat oil and fry onion slices golden brown. Add garlic cloves and fry another 1 minute till brown. Add the chicken pieces and fry a little longer till the raw colour changes and they are evenly and lightly browned. Add all the other ingredients and mix well. Cover and cook on low heat till the chicken is done and there is only a very little thick gravy. This should take about 2 hours. Alternately the curry could be cooked in the oven on med. low heat. Uncover and stir frequently, making sure the curry juices do not stick to the bottom of the pan. During cooking add just a little water only if necessary. Serve with plain boiled rice, pilau or any Indian bread.

CHICKEN CURRY (II)

6 medium red onions

8-10 cloves garlic

2 tsp. each cumin and coriander powder

1 tsp. cardamom powder

2 cups tomatoes peeled and chopped

6 whole peppercorns

2-3 whole green chillis

2½ tblsp. oil

Salt to taste

1-2" piece fresh ginger

1 large bunch fresh coriander leaves chopped

1-2 tsp. turmeric powder

4 cloves

1½-2 kg. chicken skinned and cut in serving pieces

2 bay leaves

1" piece cinnamon

1 cup more or less of water

Method

Peel and chop roughly the onions, ginger and garlic and put them all together with the coriander leaves in a blender or in a food processor. Blend or process till smooth. Heat 2 tblsp. oil. Add the blended and powdered spices. When the spices begin to stick to the bottom of the pan add the tomatoes and keep frying till there is no longer any raw smell of spices. Add the chicken pieces and continue frying till the chicken is no longer pink and is coated well with the spices. Add enough water to cover the chicken. When the curry starts boiling lower heat, cover and cook till the chicken is done. In a small fry pan heat 2 tsp oil. Add the whole spices and when they begin to splutter add to the curry. Take a little of the gravy from the curry and wash the fry pan to clear it of any oil and residue. Pour this back in the curry and stir. Add salt to taste. Also add green chillis, if using. Cook for another 4-5 minutes. Serve hot with any Indian bread, rice, or pulao, with a salad.

CHICKEN KORMA (I)

4 tblsp. oil

4 tblsp. ground onions

2 tblsp. ground garlic

1 tsp. paprika

A pinch of sugar

1 large chicken (1.5 kg.) cut in serving pieces

2 medium finely sliced, crisply fried onions for garnishing

4 hardboiled eggs cut lengthwise

2 bay leaves

2 tblsp. ground ginger

1 tsp. turmeric powder

2 tblsp. tomato purée

1 cup or more water

½ tsp. dry roasted, finely ground 'garam masala' powder

Salt to taste

Method

Warm oil in a heavy-bottomed pan. Put in the bay leaves. When it starts to splutter slightly, put in all the ground and powdered spices and fry well. When the spices start sticking to the bottom of the pan add the tomato puree, sugar, and stir. Now add the chicken pieces and fry with the spices well stirring from time to time. The chicken will be half cooked during this frying. When the chicken is well coated with the spices and a nice aroma emanates add enough water, salt, and cover to complete the cooking. If there is too much water at the end uncover the lid and dry off some of the liquid. Sprinkle garam masala powder before taking off heat. Just before serving mix the sliced eggs and the fried onions gently into the korma. Serve with rice or any type of Indian bread.

Variations:

Fish korma may be made as above. Cut 500 gm. of any good fish fillets into serving pieces. Rub salt and turmeric powder on the fish pieces and keep aside for 15 minutes or more. Heat oil, fry the fish pieces and keep aside. Add a little more oil if necessary and proceed frying the spices as the chicken korma using the following measurements: 1 bay leaf, 2 tblsp ground onion, 1 tblsp. ground ginger, 2 tsp ground garlic or less, ½ tsp paprika, ½ tsp turmeric powder and 1 tblsp. tomato purée, pinch of sugar and salt to taste, ½ tsp garam masala powder, 1 large thinly sliced and crisply fried onion and 2 hard-boiled eggs.

Add ½ cup water (a little more if necessary) after the spices have been fried well. When the water comes to the boil add the fish pieces and cook uncovered till the fish is well blended with the spices and there is a thick gravy. Be careful not to let the fish break. Now proceed like the chicken korma. Serve with rice.

CHICKEN KORMA (II)

1 cup unsweetened yogurt

4 tblsp. ground onion

Salt to taste

1 large chicken (1.54 kg.) cut in serving pieces

1" piece cinnamon

6 cloves

1 tblsp. tomato pureé (optional)

¼ tsp. saffron soaked in 1 tblsp. warm milk or water

Silver foils for garnishing

1 tblsp. good ghee (optional)

2 tblsp. ground ginger

2 tblsp. ground garlic

½ tsp. paprika

4 tblsp. oil

2 bay leaves

4 green cardamoms

4 medium onions finely sliced

Water as required

1 tblsp. rose water (optional)

Method

Beat yogurt. Add all the ground spices, paprika and salt and mix well. Marinate the chicken pieces in this mixture for ½ to 1 hr. Heat oil in a deep heavy-bottomed pan. Add the bay leaves, cinnamon, cardamoms, and cloves. When they start to splutter add half the onion slices and fry till golden brown. Add the tomato puree and mix well. When it begins to stick to the bottom of the pan quickly add the chicken with the marinade. Fry all well continuously stirring till nicely browned and there is a nice aroma. Add a little water only if necessary. Cover and cook. From time to time take off cover and stir well. Cook till chicken is done and there is only a thick gravy. During the last 5 minutes of cooking add the saffron water and cover. When ready take off heat and sprinkle rose water if using. Fry the rest of the onion slices in the ghee and mix gently into the curry. Garnish with the silver foil. Serve with rice, *pulao* or any Indian bread.

Variations:

During the last minute of cooking add 8-10 whole, well washed raisins and 6-8 blanched and slivered almonds with the saffron. No need to add the rose water.

Mutton or Beef Korma may be cooked in this manner. Hard boiled eggs can be used as garnishing like Chicken Korma –1. Use 1 kg. meat cut in medium size pieces. The rest of the ingredients should be in the same proportion as the chicken.

COLONIAL CHICKEN and EGG CURRY

2 tblsp. oil, any fat or ghee

2 large garlic clove finely crushed

2 tblsp. curry powder

1 bouillon cube

1-2 tblsp (more or less) prawn water - in which shrimp or prawn has been cooked (optional)

A pinch of monosodium glutamate or plain sugar

1-2 tblsp. (or more) coconut milk

Salt and lime juice to taste

3 heaped tblsp. minced onion

2 green chillis split and de-seeded (optional)

1 tblsp. Tomato paste or purée

1 tblsp. stock from cooked chicken

1½ kg. cooked chicken cut in serving pieces

4 hard-boiled eggs cut lengthwise in halves

1 medium onion thinly sliced and fried golden brown for garnish (optional)

Method

Heat oil. Fry the onions, garlic and chillis lightly for about 3-4 minutes. Remove from heat and add the curry powder and tomato paste. Mix thoroughly and return to low heat. Now add the bouillon cube diluted in the stock and continue to cook on low heat for another 2-3 minutes. Add prawn water and simmer gently for another couple of minutes. Add the salt and lime juice. Finally add the coconut milk. Let it come to a boil. Add the chicken pieces and let it heat through to let the curry sauce penetrate the chicken – about 1-2 minutes. Add monosodium glutamate just before taking off the heat. The gravy should not be too thick or too thin. Place on a serving dish with the eggs arranged on top. If desired serve with boiled rice. Sprinkle the top of the curry with fried onions.

Other Accompaniments: Chopped onions, tomatoes, cucumbers carrots, bamboo shoots, bananas, pineapples, a mixture of onions and chillis sultanas, coconut, peanuts, cut limes, *pappadums*, chillis (chopped or whole), bean sprouts, chutneys etc. etc.

DUM MUTTON

2 bay leaves	2 large onions thinly sliced
1 piece cinnamon (1")	4 tblsp. oil or good ghee
1 whole large brown cardamom	2 dry deseeded red chillis
4 tblsp. ground onion	4 split green cardamoms
2 tblsp. ground ginger	4-6 cloves
1 kg. mutton boneless from shoulder or leg, cut in large chunks	1 cup yogurt or, chopped peeled tomatoes
A pinch of saffron	Salt to taste

Method

Fry the sliced onions in 1 tblsp. oil, drain on paper towel and keep aside. Add the rest of the oil to the pan and warm. Add bay leaves and red dry chillis. After 1-2 minutes, add cinnamon, cardamoms, and cloves. When they start spluttering add all the ground spices. Fry well adding yoghurt or tomatoes a little at a time so that the spices do not stick to the bottom of the pan. When raw smell of spices disappears add the meat and fry well till a good healthy brownish colour. Continue adding yoghurt and tomatoes till all used. Add salt to taste. Stir well. Add saffron and fried onions (keep a handful aside for garnish) at this stage. Take off fire. Transfer all to an ovenproof dish with a tight cover and put in a moderate oven ($350°$ F) till done and most of the liquid has disappeared. Turn onto a dish, sprinkle with fried onions and cover with silver foil. Serve with any Indian bread.

Variations:

1. **Chicken Dum** can also be cooked as above. Use 1 kg. of good pieces of chicken from the leg and the shoulder. No need to bone. Use only ½ cup yoghurt or tomatoes. Proceed as above. Cooking time will also be less. Be sure not to overcook or the meat will disintegrate from the bones.
2. Whole boiled eggs cut lengthwise can be used as garnish together with the fried onions

----

MUTTON KORMA

(The korma should also be cooked on low heat to get best results)

2 kg. good mutton cubed	1 cup yogurt unsweetened
4 tblsp. oil	1-2 bay leaves
1" piece cinnamon	3-4 cloves
2-3 green whole cardamoms split	2 medium onions sliced
2 tblsp. onion ground	2 tsp. ginger ground
2 tsp. garlic ground	1 tsp. heaped cumin powder
1 tsp. heaped coriander powder	1 tsp. turmeric powder
10 raisins ground or liquidized	4 tblsp. top of milk or, thickened milk
Water as required	

Method

Marinate meat in yogurt and keep aside 30 minutes or more. Heat oil and add bay leaves, cinnamon, cloves, and cardamom. When they begin to splutter add the onion slices and fry golden. Now add all the spices including raisins and top of milk and fry well sprinkling a little water from time to time, if necessary, to prevent spices from sticking to the pan. Keep stirring on a regular basis. When the spices are all well fried and the raw smell is no longer prevalent add the marinated meat with all the juices and continue frying till meat is well browned and no longer looks raw. Add very little water, only if necessary. Cover and cook till meat is done and there is very little gravy left. Check for seasoning.

Variations:

1. Omit frying the bay leaf, cloves, cinnamon, and cardamom at the beginning. Begin the korma by frying the onion slices and continue as above. When the korma is done heat 2 tblsp. of oil or ghee in another pan and fry the whole spices. When they begin to splutter, stir into the korma. Add a bit of the hot korma juice to the pan and when it splutters again stir into the korma.

2. After frying the onions, keep them aside – they should be fried brown. When the korma is done, sprinkle a little of the fried onions into it and stir. Sprinkle the rest of the onions on top when serving.
3. Chicken or beef may be substituted instead of mutton. Turmeric could be omitted in which case the meat should be fried nice and brown without burning. All on low heat.

POSTO (WHITE POPPY SEED) MUTTON CURRY

500 gm. mutton

6 tblsp. ground onion

4 tblsp. ground garlic

2 medium onions sliced

Water as required

1 cup white poppy seed ground to a paste

4 tblsp. ground ginger

2 tblsp. oil

2 tsp. turmeric

Method

Marinate meat in the ground *posto* and half each of ground onion, ginger, and garlic for about 1-2 hrs. Heat oil. Fry sliced onions till golden add rest of ground onion, ginger and garlic and turmeric. Fry all well. Add meat with all the marinade. Cook in its own juice. Use water only if necessary. This curry should be thick with most of the liquid evaporated. It should be mushy but not dry. Serve with rice or *chapattis*, *loochis* or *parathas*.

MUTTON PRESSURE COOKER CURRY OR IN DAAB (GREEN COCONUT)

2 tblsp. oil	3 large onions sliced
1 tblsp. ground onion	2-3 tblsp. ground ginger
1 tblsp. ground garlic	2 tsp. turmeric paste or powder
1 large tomato chopped	2 kg. mutton cubed, sprinkled with turmeric and salt
1 cup unsweetened yogurt	½ tsp. paprika
Hot water for cooking as desired	1-2 green chillis split and deseeded
1" piece cinnamon	1 large whole cardamom or, 4 green whole cardamoms
4-5 cloves	4-5 whole black peppercorns
1 large pinch saffron	Green coconut (*daab*) (optional)

Method

Heat oil. Fry onions till golden. Add all the ground ingredients, turmeric, and tomatoes. When all are well fried add the meat and 2 tblsp. yoghurt. The meat must be fried well till all liquid disappears. Now place all in a pressure cooker with very little water, green chillis and paprika and cook for 15mins to ½ hr. depending on the toughness of the meat.

In another saucepan heat the rest of the yoghurt with the cinnamon, cardamom, cloves, peppercorns, till the oil separates from the yogurt. Pour this into the meat mixture and heat a little more till well mixed. Take off heat and transfer to a serving dish. Mix the saffron with a little hot water and pour over the meat.

Meat in Daab

Cut the top of the *daab* and reserve. Pour out the coconut water. Take out the tender scrapings from inside the coconut which can be mixed with the meat or kept aside for other use. Now cook the meat as above. Do not put in the pressure cooker. Instead put the meat in the *daab*. Cover with the top and seal well with a little dough. Either put on top of the cooker on a skillet or cook in a moderate oven. 15 minutes to ½ hour. When done let cool. Take out from the coconut and proceed with the yogurt and saffron as above. If desired when the meat is ready, it may be returned to the *daab* and served.

MUTTON CURRY

(This curry should be cooked on low heat to get best results)

2 kg. mutton cut in large cubes	1 cup unsweetened yogurt
4 tblsp. oil	3-4 medium onions cut in slices
4-5 large cloves garlic	2 tsp. ginger ground
2 tsp. freshly roasted cumin powder	2 tsp. freshly roasted coriander powder
1 tsp. heaped turmeric powder	4-5 large potatoes in their jackets, washed and well-scrubbed
2 tblsp. good ghee	½ cup water
Salt to taste	1 tsp. freshly ground garam masala

Method

Marinate meat in yogurt and keep aside for 30 minutes or more. Heat oil and fry onions. Next add garlic and fry a little. Add ginger, cumin, coriander and turmeric and fry some more about 5-8 minutes. Now add the meat and keep frying stirring from time to time. Middle of the frying process add the potatoes and keep frying till there is a nice aroma of fried spices and no raw smell left. Add sufficient water, let all come to a boil, cover, and cook till meat and potatoes are done. There should be very little gravy left in the pan, just sufficient to cover the meat and potatoes. Add salt. When curry is done uncover and leave on top of the stove. At this juncture warm the ghee and fry the garam masala in it. Put a bit of the curry gravy in it and then turn out the whole into the main curry, stir a couple of minutes. Remove from heat and serve with rice, pulao, or any Indian bread. This should be accompanied with any Indian salad or a curried vegetable.

Variations:

This curry may be cooked in the pressure cooker which will take less time and save on fuel. In this case additional water may not be necessary as enough water will come out the meat. Once the meat is done continue as above with the ghee and garam masala by opening the cover of the cooker.

SAAG MEAT

1 kg. spinach	A pinch of sodium bicarbonate
1 tblsp. gram flour (*besan*) or plain white flour	2 tblsp. oil
2 medium tomatoes chopped	2 medium onions finely sliced
1-2 green chillis optional	Salt to taste

Mutton curry

2 tblsp. oil	1 whole dry red chilli -- deseeded
1 bay leaf	1 medium onion sliced
2 tblsp. onion paste	2 tsp. each ginger and garlic paste
1 tsp. each, coriander, and cumin powder	1 tsp. turmeric powder
2 tblsp. yogurt or 2 medium tomatoes chopped	300-400 gm. good mutton cut in cubes
½ tsp. *garam masala* powder dry-roasted on a grill	

Method

Boil or steam spinach with a pinch of sodium bicarbonate to get the bitterness of the spinach out. When cool liquidize spinach with gram flour. The gram flour is added to ensure the water in the spinach does not separate. Heat oil. Fry onions golden and then add the chopped tomatoes. Fry a little till well blended with the onions. Now add the spinach and cook for a little while till mushy, and the raw smell of gram flour disappears. Add salt according to taste and green chillis. Spinach is naturally salty so be careful when adding salt. Keep aside till the meat curry is ready.

Heat oil. Add chilli and bay leaf. When they begin to splutter, add and fry onion until golden. Now add all the pastes and powders. Fry well adding yogurt and tomatoes. When a nice aroma emanates, add the meat, and again fry well. Add just enough warm water to cook the meat. Dry off excess liquid and then add to the spinach. Cook the whole for a few more minutes longer till the saag and meat are well blended. When Saag Meat is ready sprinkle *garam masala* powder on top and serve.

Alternately, cook the mutton according to your favourite recipe and add to the spinach.

GOAN LIVER CURRY

2 tblsp. oil	2 large onions sliced in rounds
2 large tomatoes chopped	2 tblsp. chopped fresh coriander leaves
½ tsp. turmeric powder	1½ tsp. North Indian 'garam masala' powder
1 tblsp. ground ginger	½ tsp. or more chilli powder (optional)
1 tblsp. ground garlic	2 tblsp. tomato purée
500 gm. liver sliced	½ cup warm water (optional)
Juice of 1 lime	Salt to taste

Method

Heat oil. Fry sliced onions. When well browned, add tomatoes and fry some more till squashy. Now add the coriander leaves, the ground and powdered spices and tomato puree. Fry all for about 5 minutes and then add the liver slices. Allow to cook in its own gravy. Add warm water only if necessary. Check seasoning when nearly done before taking off heat. When liver is cooked add the lime juice. Take off heat and serve with boiled rice. Garnish with a sprinkle of coriander leaves and green chillis. Do not overcook liver especially, if not using water as instead of getting soft it gets dry and tough.

LAMB or BEEF MINCE KEBABS IN YOGURT

1 kg. meat -- ground very fine

1 tsp. heaped garlic paste (optional)

2 tsp. coriander powder

5-6 green chillis (optional)

1 egg

1 cup oil (more or less)

2 cups unsweetened yogurt

2 tsp. heaped onion paste

1 tsp. heaped ginger paste

2 tsp. cumin powder

Salt and pepper to taste

2 slices of bread soaked in water

1-2 tblsp good ghee or, butter

1 bunch fresh coriander leaves for garnish

Method

Mix meat, onion, ginger, garlic pastes, 1 tsp each coriander and cumin powders, 1-2 green chillis, if using, minced fine with or without seeds, salt and pepper to taste, egg, and bread (after squeezing out the water). Shape into small flat burgers like *shammi* kebabs 1" in diameter. Fry the kebabs in just enough oil to cover in a deep flat heavy bottomed pan. Fry 6-8 at a time on medium to slow heat after initially heating the oil. The temperature of the oil should be controlled carefully or else the kebabs will remain raw inside with the outside browning quickly. Drain on paper towel.

Melt ghee/butter and pour into 1 or 2 ovenproof dishes. Lay the kebabs in the dish. They should not overlap. Beat yogurt with a little salt (if desired) and pour over the kebabs. Sprinkle the rest of the freshly roasted and ground cumin and coriander powders on top. Lay a few whole green chillis also on top. Cook in a pre-heated moderate oven for about 20 minutes. The yogurt should set and resemble poached egg. Sprinkle chopped coriander leaves before serving. Serve with any Indian bread and *raita* or salad.

Variation: For that additional touch warm 1 tsp ghee or butter. Add 1-2 tsp. Kashmiri *mirch*, *degi mirch* or paprika. When smoking but not burnt, pour over the kebabs along with the coriander and cumin powders before placing in the oven. Alternatively, the yogurt could be flavoured with a few strands of saffron. Rose water could be sprinkled on top just before removing from the oven.

CURRIED BEEF and PUMPKIN

1 tblsp. oil
200 gm. red pumpkin cubed
Water as required
1-2 dry red chilli de-seeded (optional)
1 large onion coarsely sliced
1-2 medium potatoes cubed small
1-2 tsp. Worcestershire sauce

½ tsp. black cumin seed
1 tsp. turmeric powder
1 bay leaf
250 gm. fillet cut in thin strips
125 gm. spring onion chopped
1 tsp. each coriander and cumin powder

Method

Heat 1 tblsp. oil and add the black cumin seeds. When they begin to splutter add the pumpkin and turmeric powder and fry for a few minutes. Add just enough water and pressure cook till soft. Next heat the rest of the oil in a non-stick pan and add the bay leaf and whole red chilli. When the latter starts browning add and fry fillet strips briskly with onions, spring onions and potatoes. Dry roast the coriander and cumin powders on a griddle to bring out the aroma. Add this along with the Worcestershire sauce to the meat mixture. Cook till the potatoes are soft. Add the pumpkin mixture to the meat mixture. Stir and cook for a few minutes more till well mixed and mushy. Garnish with fresh green chillis, coriander leaves and a sprinkle of dry roasted cumin powder. Serve with chapattis or any other Indian bread

This is a good way to stretch a dish if unexpected visitors drop in!

Note

1 tsp. heaped dry roasted curry powder can replace the coriander and cumin powders when cooking the meat mixture.

The potato cubes can be cooked with the pumpkin mixture rather than the meat mixture. The beef fillet strips will cook very fast.

The beef can be substituted with thin mutton or chicken strips though the beef fillet strips bring out the best in this dish!

VEGETARIAN CURRIES AND LENTILS

PAPAYA DALNA

500 gm. green papaya cut in small cubes

Water as required

1 tsp. turmeric

2 green chillis seeded and slit

2 tsp. oil

½ tsp. white whole cumin seeds

Salt to taste

¼ tsp. sugar

Method

Steam papaya till half done. Heat oil. Add cumin seeds. When seeds begin to splutter add the papaya and fry gently for 3 or 4 minutes. Now add a little water, salt to taste, sugar, turmeric and green chillis. Let it cook till mushy. Serve with rice and dal, and chapattis.

Variation:

Chickpeas, shrimps, or small cubed potatoes may be added. They could be added individually or as a combination of two or all three. Lightly fry these ingredients before adding to the papaya.

GREEN PAPAYA DRY CURRY

1-2 tblsp. oil

1 tsp. ginger paste

½ tsp. turmeric powder

1 cup thick coconut milk

1-2 green chillis whole

2 tsp. onion paste

1 tsp. garlic paste

500 gm. green papaya finely grated

Salt to taste

Method

Heat oil. Fry all the spices until there is no raw smell. Add the papaya, stir and cook for 2-3 minutes. Add the coconut milk and salt. Keep cooking till it becomes fairly dry and is of a mushy consistency. Add the chillis when dish is almost ready.

MA'S GREEN PAPAYA GHONTO or DRY CURRY

3-4 tblsp. oil
½ tsp. whole black cumin seeds
1 tsp. turmeric paste
500 gm. green papaya cut small
Salt to taste
10-15 *"Boris"*

25 gm. potato cut small
1 tsp. ginger paste
1 tsp. white cumin paste
1-2 fresh green or dry red chillis
A pinch of sugar
½ cup or less water

Method

Heat oil, fry the potato cubes drain and keep aside. Add a little more oil if necessary. Put in the whole black cumin seeds. When they begin to splutter add all the spices and dry chilli, if used. Fry well. Now add the papaya and potato. Fry well with the spices. Add green chilli if used, salt to taste, sugar, and very little water. Keep cooking till curry is done. Just before taking off the heat add the *boris*, mix well and cook for another 2-3 minutes.

Boris: Soak ½ cup red lentils (*masur dal*) in enough water to cover overnight. Next morning throw away any excess water and liquidize to a fine paste. Add salt to taste, 1 small finely chopped green chilli minus the seeds and 1 very small finely minced onion (optional). Heat 4 tblsp. oil in a small wok. Drop the batter in coffee spoonfuls. Fry golden. Drain and keep aside till required.

CAULIFLOWER and POTATO KALIA (BENGALI)

1 cup unsweetened yogurt well beaten

4 tblsp. ground onion

2 tsp. ground ginger

1 tsp. ground garlic

Pinch sugar

Salt to taste

¼ tsp. paprika or, red chilli powder

500 gm. cauliflower washed well and cut into medium sized florets

250 gm. potatoes cut in cubes to match the size of cauliflowers

4-6 tblsp. oil

125 gm. onion thinly sliced

2 whole cloves

2 cardamoms

Water as required

Method

Beat yogurt well. Add all fresh ground spices, sugar, salt, and red paprika. Mix well and marinate potatoes and cauliflower in it for about 2 hours making sure the paste penetrates the crevices of the cauliflower. Heat oil. Fry sliced onions brown. Add whole cloves, cardamoms, and cinnamon. When they start to splutter add all the vegetables with the marinade. Cook gently till a nice aroma emanates. Add water only if necessary. Cover vegetables and cook on low heat till vegetables are done and the gravy is thick. It should have a nice brownish red colour.

Variation:

The potatoes in the above recipe may be omitted and the cauliflower kept whole. The marinate must be spread over the cauliflower and inserted into the gaps and crevices well. Cook gently as above keeping the cauliflower whole in a large deep pan till done. The cauliflower can also be cooked in a moderate oven. After 2 hours take cauliflower out of the marinade and brown those on top of the cooker gently. Place in a baking dish and cover with the scraping of the pan and the rest of the marinade. Add a little water only if necessary. Cover and bake till done.

GUJARATI PEAS and CAULIFLOWER CURRY

½ cup tender fresh, dehydrated or canned green peas

1 medium cauliflower with the florets cut very small.

1-2 tblsp. oil

½ tsp. whole mustard seeds

½ tsp. crushed asafœtida

1 tsp. turmeric powder

Salt to taste

2-3 fresh green chillis (optional)

½ cup or less water

Method

Heat oil and fry the cauliflower for 3-4 minutes. Add the peas and fry another 2 minutes. Add all the other ingredients and very little water. Stir well and cook for a couple of minutes. Cover and cook for only a few more minutes till ready. Omit the turmeric for a white curry.

BEET GHONTO (BENGALI)

2 tblsp. oil

2 large potatoes diced

3 bay leaves

½ tsp. ginger paste

½ tsp. coriander powder

1-2 tsp. melted ghee (optional)

½ tsp. *panchphoron*

500 gm. beetroot grated

½ tsp. cumin powder

Salt to taste

1-2 split green chillis (optional)

Fresh coriander leaves chopped for garnish

Method

Heat oil. Add the *panchphoron*. When it begins to splutter add the potatoes and fry till golden, 5-10 minutes. Add the beet root and all the other ingredients except the chillis, ghee and coriander leaves. Stir the mixture well to blend. Cover and cook till the water from the beet root dries up and the potatoes are done. Add the green chillis just before the dish is ready. Let it cook for another couple of minutes. Take off heat and turn into a serving dish. Sprinkle ghee on top and stir gently. Garnish with the coriander. This dish should be a dry mushy consistency without the potatoes breaking up. Serve as a vegetable accompaniment with any Indian preferably Bengali meal.

SHEEM (BROAD BEANS) PATURI – BENGALI

2 tblsp. white mustard seeds

2 tsp. grated coconut

2-3 tblsp. oil

500 gm. *sheem* with top and bottom snipped off

½ tsp. mustard oil (optional)

1-2 green chillis (or according to taste de-seeded)

1-2 tsp. turmeric paste

½ tsp. black cumin seeds

Salt to taste

Fresh coriander leaves chopped for garnish

Method

Grind the mustard seeds, chilli, and coconut together into a paste. Heat oil, add the black cumin seeds. When they begin to splutter add the *sheem* and stir. Add the pastes and all the other ingredients except the mustard oil and coriander leaves. Stir to mix and cover. Cook till done. The gravy should be thick. Just before taking off heat sprinkle the mustard oil and cook for another couple of mins. Turn out into a serving dish and garnish with the coriander leaves.

SHUKTO (I) – BENGALI STARTER

(This is a very popular starter to any Bengali meal and can be termed as an appetizer. A very light curry, which is meant to be good for the health. There are many versions and combinations of this famous dish. Usually the addition of *karela* (bitter gourd) is a must.)

4-5 broad beans	1 large white radish
4-5 medium bitter gourd (*karela*)	1 large aubergine
5-6 medium potatoes	1-2 drumsticks
½ cup shelled peas	2 tblsp. oil
A pinch black cumin seed (kalonji)	A pinch fenugreek seeds
A pinch white cumin seeds	A pinch whole black mustard seeds
A pinch fennel seeds	1" piece ginger ground fine
2 tsp. finely ground black mustard powder or paste	1 tsp. turmeric paste or powder
A pinch sugar	Salt to taste
Water as required	1 tblsp. milk

Method

Cut all vegetables lengthwise. Heat oil in a wok. Put all whole spices in. When they start to splutter add all the vegetables. Sauté a little. Add all the ground spices sugar and salt. Mix well and enough water to cook the vegetables. When vegetables are done and the excess water evaporates add milk and cook a little till gravy is thick.

LAU (WHITE GOURD) OR VEGETABLE SHUKTO (II)

1-2 tblsp. oil

1 large or, 2 medium carrots cut in chunks

1-2 green bananas cubed

1 large or, 2 medium radishes cut in chunks

1 tsp. freshly roasted coriander powder

2 tsp. ghee

Salt to taste

1½ cup coconut milk or, just plain fresh milk

2-3 small *karelas* cut in chunks

1 large aubergine cut in chunky cubes

2 medium potatoes cut in small cubes

¼ cup yogurt

1½ tsp. freshly roasted cumin powder

Water as required

¼ tsp. sugar

Method

Heat oil in a pan and fry the karela pieces for a few minutes. Add all the other vegetables with the yoghurt and spices reserving ½ tsp cumin powder. Fry all for 5-10 minutes till all well mixed. Now add some water and the coconut milk. Next add the sugar and the salt. Cook for another 20-25 minutes till the gravy is thick and vegetables are done. Add the ghee just before taking off the heat. Sprinkle with the ½ tsp cumin powder and serve with plain boiled rice.

SHUKTO (III) AS A VARIATION TO (I) or (II)

2-4 tblsp. oil (preferably mustard oil)

2-3 potatoes cubed

1 large sweet potato cubed

3-4 green French beans cut in ½" lengths

1-2 bitter gourds (*karelas*) sliced

1 large green banana cut in half and each quartered

¼-½ tsp. *panchphoron*

½-1 tsp. ginger paste

½-1 tsp. coriander powder

½-1 tsp. turmeric powder

½-1 tsp. mustard paste

1-2 green chillis split and deseeded

½ tsp. chilli powder (optional)

Salt to taste

1 bay leaf

Method

Sauté or deep fry all the above vegetables and keep aside. Remove excess oil leaving just 1 tsp. in the pan. Add the bay leaf and *panchphoron*. When the seeds begin to splutter add all the spices and fry well. Add the vegetables, chillis, chilli powder and salt and stir to mix well with the spices. Cover and cook. Add a little water only if necessary. The gravy should be thick so avoid adding water if possible.

BENGALI LABRA OR MIXED VEGETABLE CURRY

1 tblsp. oil	½ tsp. *panchphoron*
2 tsp. ginger powder	500 gm. assorted vegetables cut in cubes**
4-5 large potatoes cut in cubes	Salt to taste
½ tsp. turmeric powder	½ tsp. freshly ground cumin powder
½ tsp. freshly ground coriander powder	A pinch red chilli powder (optional)
¼ tsp. fennel powder	1 tblsp. good ghee (optional)
A pinch sugar	Water as required

**An assortment of either, winter or, summer vegetables are advisable. Try not to use a combination of the two, e.g. brinjals, green bananas, drumsticks (cut lengthwise), red pumpkins, okra (also cut lengthwise), sweet potatoes etc. or, carrots, green beans (cut lengthwise), beetroot, cauliflower, turnips, cabbage (cut in squares) etc.

Method

Warm oil in a wok. Put in '*panchphoron*'. When spluttering starts, add the ginger and, sauté for a minute. Add all the vegetables including potatoes. Fry all well. Add turmeric, cover, and cook. Add water only if required. When ready add salt, stir. Add the rest of the powdered spices and sugar. Stir well. Add ghee just before taking off the heat.

BENGALI VEGETABLE CURRY OR DALNA

500 gm. potatoes

200 gm. *patal (palwal)*

2 tblsp. mustard oil or substitute

1 tsp. whole cumin seeds

1 tsp. thinly sliced ginger

2 tsp. white poppy seed

2 tblsp. unsweetened yogurt

Salt to taste

½ tsp. mixture of freshly powdered cloves, cinnamon and cardamom

1 tblsp. pure ghee

200 gm. cauliflower

200 gm. cabbage

2 bay leaves

2-3 green chillis split and deseeded

1 tsp. aniseed *(sonf)*

1-2 dry chillis deseeded (optional)

Pinch sugar

2 tsp. turmeric powder or paste

Water for cooking the vegetables

Method

Wash and cut all vegetables the same size. Heat oil and sauté the vegetable brown. Keep aside. Add all the spices, yoghurt and seasoning and stir till well mixed. Cook for about 5 minutes. When a pleasant smell emanates add enough water to cook the vegetables. Do not add too much water – just about half cover the vegetables. Cook till all done and the gravy is thick. Add more water only if required. Always add hot water. When done add the ghee and sprinkle the *garam masala* powder. Give a quick stir just once. Take off heat and serve with rice or chapattis.

Variations:

1. The above *dalna* can be made with potatoes and just one vegetable such as either cauliflower, *patal*, aubergine, or cabbage etc.
2. It can also be made as follows: Heat oil and sauté potatoes till golden. Take off heat. In the same oil add 2 whole bay leaves, 4 cloves, 2-3 cardamoms, 1" cinnamon and 2 dry deseeded red chillis (optional). When spices begin to splutter add the vegetables and sauté well. for about 2-3 minutes. Add 1 tsp. ginger juice, ½ tsp. powdered cumin, ½ tsp. powdered coriander, 1 tsp. turmeric powder, pinch sugar, and salt

to taste. Mix all well and cook for about 5 minutes till raw smell of spices disappear. Add enough water to cook vegetables and leave a thickish gravy. During the last minute of cooking add 1-2 split deseeded if desired. Green chillis give a good flavour.

3. If a white *dalna* is required omit the turmeric powder and increase the cumin and coriander powders by ½ tsp each. A white cauliflower and potato *dalna* is especially good. Can add 8-10 whole raisins well washed and sticks taken out, at the same time as the green chillis. If raisins are added, cut out the pinch of sugar.

MIXED VEGETABLES WITH MUSTARD AND COCONUT

4-5 beet roots	4-5 carrots
1 medium cauliflower	2-3 potatoes
Salt to taste	1 tblsp. white mustard paste made freshly from white mustard seeds
1-2 fresh green chillis slit	1 cup fresh tender green peas
2-3 tblsp. mustard oil	1 tblsp. grated coconut
2 tblsp. turmeric paste	

Method

Cut the beet roots, carrots, cauliflower, and potatoes into small pieces. Mix all the vegetables with salt, mustard, and turmeric paste. Add the green chillis. Pour the oil in and gently toss to mix. Now steam all preferably in a steamer or pressure cooker about 5-10 minutes. When ready dry off on medium heat. Add the coconut, stir for a couple of minutes before removing from heat. Serve with rice or any Indian bread.

Variation:

1. One or more of all the vegetables can be substituted with any of the following– radish, cabbage, turnip, green beans, kohlrabi etc. etc.
2. Groundnut oil may be used instead of mustard oil. The latter gives a better flavour.

VEGETABLE PATURI (BENGALI BANANA LEAF WRAPPED SMOKED VEGETABLE DRY CURRY)

1 medium snake gourd peeled and chopped

500 gm. pumpkin chopped

3-4 carrots peeled and chopped

1-2 onions chopped

½ cup (more or less) wheat flour

2-4 tblsp. mustard oil

3-4 fresh green chillis

2 large banana leaves

4-6 *patals* (*palwal* – Indian vegetable) seeded and chopped

4-6 okras chopped

¼ cup green peas

1 cup coconut flakes

2 tsp. turmeric powder

2 tblsp. black mustard paste

Salt to taste

Method

Mix all the vegetables and salt. Bind with the wheat flour. Add all the rest of the ingredients and wrap in the washed banana leaves like a parcel securing well so that the contents do not spill out. Place parcel on a griddle (*tawa*) and cook over medium heat. When one side of the packet begins to char turn over and cook the other side similarly. When the parcel is done (leaves should have a burnt appearance) a smoky smell will emanate. Take off heat and carefully open the parcel. Turn the vegetable onto a serving dish and serve with rice, lentils (*dal*) or any Indian bread.

Note. An assortment of vegetables of any kind including potatoes may be used for this dish. Try not to break up the brinjals.

METHI ALOO (FENUGREEK POTATOES)

2 tsp. oil

½ tsp. fenugreek seeds

1 kg. methi sag (fresh fenugreek leaves)

1 dry chilli de-seeded

500 gm. very small potatoes peeled and kept whole

Salt to taste

Method

Warm oil in pan. Add dry chilli and then the fenugreek seeds. When they start to splutter add the potatoes. Keep frying till nearly done. Add the *methi* sag, stir and cover. Cook till done adding salt to taste. It should be dryish with the sag adhering to the potatoes. The water from the sag should disappear.

For a quicker method half boil the potatoes before proceeding as above. Serve with chapattis.

ALOO BATI-CHORCHORI

(This is another light and popular Bengali dish. It really means a spiced steamed dryish potato curry)

3-4 medium potatoes cut very small	1 tsp. turmeric
2 fresh green chillis split and deseeded	2 tsp. oil
1-2 tblsp. water	2 tblsp. green peas (optional)
1 small onion minced (optional)	½ tsp. ginger minced (optional)

Method

Combine all the above ingredients, cover, and cook on low heat. It will cook in its own steam. Alternately pressure cook by putting all the ingredients in a covered bowl inside the cooker. Can also use a steamer putting contents in a covered bowl in which case no water should be added to the potatoes. The water in the cooker or steamer is enough to cook the *chorchori*. This is served with rice and lentils or any Indian bread.

Variations:

1. Any of the optional items above may be omitted.
2. 1 medium carrot cut very small can be added with the peas.
3. Instead of ginger use ½ tsp whole black cumin seeds.
4. Put all the ingredients in a heat-proof dish with cover and microwave for 5-8 minutes at power 7.
5. Use 3-4 cloves of garlic or ½ tsp. garlic powder instead of onions and ginger.

MA'S ALOO POSTO (POTATO WITH POPPY SEED PASTE) (I)

(The above is an ever-popular dish of Bengal. This is a simple version from my Mother-in-law. She was never a great cook but had a few pet recipes which were simple and delicious!)

1-2 tblsp. oil	1 large onion sliced finely
250 gm. potatoes cut in cubes	3-4 tblsp. poppy seeds liquidized into a fine paste
½-1 tsp. turmeric powder	¼ cup or more water
1-2 whole green chillis	Salt to taste

Method

Heat oil. Fry onions till golden. Add the potatoes and fry till golden brown. Next add the poppy seed paste and turmeric and salt. Mix all well and keep cooking till done. Add water as required only if necessary. Add the chillis a few minutes before taking off the heat. When done the potatoes should be well coated in the paste but remain soft and whole.

POTATO and POPPY SEED DRY CURRY
(ALOO POSTO) (II)

6 tblsp. poppy seeds soaked overnight

¼ tsp. *panchphoron**

½ tsp. turmeric powder

Salt to taste

2 tblsp. oil

4-5 medium potatoes cubed small

1 small green chilli

Water as required

Method

Make a paste of the poppy seed in the food processor or liquidizer. Keep aside. Heat oil and put in the *panchphoron*. When it starts to splutter add the potatoes and fry till slightly brown. Add the turmeric and green chilli and stir to mix. Now add the poppy seed paste and the water. Stir continuously and be careful not to let curry get burnt. Poppy seed paste burns easily.

Variation:

The '*panchphoron*' may be omitted. Add 2-3 zucchinis cut in thin rings with the potatoes.

STEAMED POTATOES WITH POPPY SEED PASTE (III)

250. gm. small round potatoes   or 1 large or 2 medium potatoes sliced

4 tblsp. poppy seed paste   2-3 whole green chillis

2-3 tblsp. mustard oil   1 tsp. turmeric

Salt to taste

Method

Mix all together and steam in a steamer, pressure cooker, rice cooker or in a double boiler till potatoes are done. Those who are allergic to the smell of mustard oil can substitute any other oil. However, the mustard oil brings out the real flavour of this dish!

ALOO POSTO (POTATO POPPY SEED CURRY) (IV)

½-¾ cup white poppy seeds soaked in enough water to cover over night

1-2 tblsp. oil

½-1 tsp. turmeric powder

500 gm. potatoes cut in small cubes

½-1 cup water or, as required

Salt to taste

1-2 green chillis (optional)

Method

Liquidise posto to a fine paste. Heat oil. Smear potato cubes with turmeric and a little salt and fry till a brown colour. Add the posto paste, whole split or sliced green chillis and enough water, as necessary. Add salt to taste. Keep cooking till potatoes are done and the curry reaches a mushy consistency.

Variation:

1-2 onions and 100 gm. or more shrimps may be added to the above curry. Cut onion in large slices and together with the shrimps fry with the potatoes.

HING ALOO-DUM (POTATO WITH ASAFŒTIDA)

3 tblsp. oil

½ tsp. whole cumin seeds

1 tsp. cumin powder

1 tsp. ginger paste

Salt to taste

1-2 green chillis

½ tsp. ground asafœtida

4-5 large potatoes cut in large serving cubes

1 tsp. turmeric powder

½ tsp. sugar

1 cup water

Method

Heat oil. Add asafœtida and whole cumin seeds. When they start to splutter add the potatoes and fry a golden brown. Add all the spices, sugar, and salt. Fry all well stirring continuously. Add water and chilli to cook the potatoes. Add more water if necessary. This should have a thickish gravy just about coating the potatoes. Serve with *puris*.

STELLAMASHI'S SORSE ALOO
(POTATOES IN MUSTARD SAUCE)

500 gm. potatoes cubed small

¼ tsp. whole mustard seeds

2 tblsp. unsweetened yogurt

Salt to taste

1-2 tblsp. oil

2 tsp. freshly ground mustard paste

1-2 whole split green chillis

Method

Boil potatoes. Heat oil and add the mustard seeds. When the seeds begin to splutter add the potatoes and fry well. Add the mustard paste (if desired, diluted in very little water and strained). Stir all well and cook for a few minutes till potatoes are well coated. just before taking off the heat add the beaten yogurt. Mix well. Add the chillis and salt to taste. Stir all till well blended. Sprinkle melted ghee over the whole. Serve with rice or any Indian bread.

MUMMY'S ALOO DUM (DRY POTATO CURRY)

2 tblsp. oil

2 large onions ground to paste

1 tsp. turmeric powder

2 tblsp. raisins

2 tblsp. vinegar

2 bay leaves

2 tsp. ginger paste

½ tsp. red chilli powder (optional)

1 kg. small potatoes half boiled and peeled

1-2 tsp. sugar

Method

Heat oil, in a heavy-bottomed or a non-stick pan. Add the bay leaves. Next add onion and ginger paste, turmeric, and chilli powder. Fry all well sprinkling a little water at a time so that the spices do not stick to the bottom of the pan. Once the spices are well fried and there is a nice smell, add the raisins and potatoes, stirring to let all the ingredients mix well. Add very little water to just cook the potatoes and to make sure the spices do not remain raw. Mix the vinegar, sugar and salt and pour over the cooked *aloo dum*. Sprinkle with garam masala powder before taking off the heat. Garnish with chopped coriander leaves. Serve with *puris* or any other Indian bread. The curry should have a scant thick gravy.

Variations:

1. If very small potatoes are not available, then cut medium potatoes in half after boiling and peeling.
2. The vinegar, sugar, salt mixture could be added with the spices at the beginning and then fried. After that, add the raisins, fry, and then add the potatoes and enough water to cook.
3. Instead of vinegar ¼-½ cup unsweetened yogurt may be added while frying the spices. At this time 1-2 tblsp. tomato purée may also be added.

SPICY BRINJAL

4 tbsp. oil	500 gm. med. slim brinjal cut in fours
2-4 tablsp. onion paste	2-3 tsp. ginger paste
2-3 tsp. garlic paste	2 tblsp' mustard paste
2 tasp. turmeric powder	Salt to taste
1 tsp. sugar	1 tblsp. or more vinegar

Method

Heat oil and fry the brinjals just to soften and change colour. Drain and keep aside. Next fry the onion, ginger and garlic pastes well. Add mustard paste and turmeric. and fry for a min. Now add the salt, sugar, and vinegar to get a sweet and sour taste. When the mixture starts to bubble lay the fried brinjals carefully on top. From time-to-time spoon some of the gravy on top of the brinjals. Cook till the brinjals are done and the spices have penetrated. When ready the brinjals should have a thick spicy gravy. Serve with puris!

AUBERGINE (BEGUN) KALANJI

(This is one of my mother's favourite recipes and has always been very popular with family and friends. The irony is that she always disliked aubergine and yet concocted a recipe such as this. However, I don't ever remember her ever having it herself. My mother very seldom believed in accurate measurements – they were always very vague. All the same the end result was always out of this world. Another secret – she cooked the "*kalanji*" in pure ghee. I have however added the ghee at the end for that extra flavour due to our modern-day health concerns. I have also given an approximate measurement of ingredients. More or less of the same may be used.)

2-4 tblsp. oil

2-3 bay leaves

2-4 large onion sliced

4 tblsp. liquidized onion

1 tblsp. liquidized fresh ginger

1 tsp. turmeric powder

1 tsp. each cumin and coriander powder freshly roasted

Chilli powder to taste

1 kg. aubergine cut in 2" × 3" pieces

1 tblsp. vinegar

1 tsp. sugar

Salt to taste

1-2 tblsp. raisins washed and de-stemmed

1-2 tsp. pure ghee

½ cup water or more as required

Method

Heat oil in a wide shallow saucepan or in a fry pan. Fry bay leaves and sliced onions till red. Add all the liquidized and dry powders. Fry all well, sprinkling a little water from time to time so that the spices do not stick to the bottom. When the spices are fried to a red colour and there is a pleasant aroma, lay the aubergine slices on the spices gently. Do not place the aubergines on top of each other. Fry the aubergine well with the spices by placing some of the spices on top. When one side is done turn them over gently and keep frying. Add a little water if too dry. Cover and cook till aubergines are done. The gravy should be thick with the spices floating on top separated from the oil.

In a bowl mix the vinegar, sugar, salt, and raisins. Pour over the thick curry. Let it cook for a couple of minutes. As soon as the dish is taken off the heat sprinkle the ghee over it. Serve garnished with chopped fresh coriander leaves if desired, with rice or any kind of Indian bread – chapattis are the best bet.

COCONUT BRINJAL

2-4 tblsp. oil

250 gm (or more) onions chopped

Salt to taste

A pinch of sugar

2-3 green chillis (optional)

1 tsp. black cumin seeds

500 gm. small, long brinjals cut in half lengthwise

1-2 tblsp. mustard paste freshly ground (optional)

½ cup coconut grated

1-2 tsp. turmeric powder (optional)

Method

Heat oil over low flame in a large fry pan. Put the black cumin seeds and when they begin to splutter add the onions. When the onions become transparent add the brinjals smeared with turmeric, if using, and salt. Fry brinjals gently and when almost ready add the mustard paste, if using. Cook for a couple of minutes. Now add the grated coconut, salt, sugar and chillis. Cook for another 2-3 minutes. Take off heat and serve as an accompaniment with any Indian meal or just plain rice or any Indian bread.

Note: The turmeric may be added at the same time as the mustard paste instead of smearing the brinjals with it. One dry red chilli can be added with the black cumin seeds. Try not to break up the brinjals.

MA'S WHITE PUMPKIN (*CHAAL KUMRA*) CURRY

1½-2 kg. pumpkin shredded and steamed

1-1½ tsp. ginger paste

1-2 tblsp. fresh grated coconut

A pinch of sugar

Salt to taste

1-2 tblsp. oil

1 tsp. whole black cumin seeds

1 tsp. turmeric powder

1-2 fresh green chillis split

Method

Squeeze out all the water from the pumpkin. Heat oil. Put in the black cumin seeds. When they begin to splutter add the pumpkin and all the other ingredients and cook stirring frequently till slightly mushy and dry. Serve with rice and dal (lentils.) as a vegetable accompaniment.

PIQUANT GREEN JACK FRUIT (ENCHORE) CURRY

500 gm. *enchore* cut in cubes

2 tsp. *panchphoron*

1-2 green chillis minced

¼ cup yogurt beaten

A pinch of sugar

2 tsp. ghee melted

3 tblsp. oil

1 tblsp. fresh ginger minced

4 tblsp. freshly ground mustard paste

Salt to taste

1 tblsp. mustard oil

Method

Boil the *echore*, drain the water and discard. In the meantime, heat oil and add *panchphoron*, ginger and chilli all together. When the *panchphoron* begins to splutter add the *echore* and fry slightly for about 4-5 minutes. Add the mustard paste. Fry well till *echore* turns a nice brown colour and the oil and mustard paste blends together into one whole mass. Take off heat and cool. Add the curd, salt and sugar and mix gently. Pour the mustard oil on top and stir slightly to mix. (If the smell of raw mustard oil is too overpowering then heat the oil to burning point.) Pour into a serving bowl and sprinkle ghee before serving. This dish can be served with any Indian meal or with plain boiled rice or any Indian bread.

KANCHKALA OR GREEN BANANA CURRY

6-7 green bananas or *kanchkalas*

1-2 bay leaves

2 tblsp. onion paste

1 tsp. garlic paste

1-2 tsp. turmeric powder

2-3 ripe tomatoes chopped

Salt to taste

½ tsp. Bengali *garam masala* powder

2 tblsp. oil

2 onions sliced thinly

2 tsp. ginger paste

1 tsp. each coriander and cumin powder

½ cup unsweetened yogurt

2 cups warm water

2-3 fresh green chillis

1-2 tblsp. coriander leaves chopped

Method

Make the '*kachkala*' burghers as in "Tea Time Snacks" in this book. Make the burgers slightly smaller or into koftas for the curry and omit the chopped green chillis. The addition of paprika is optional.

For the curry – heat oil. Add bay leaves and sliced onions. When the onions turn golden brown add all the spices except *garam masala* and fry well adding yogurt a little at a time. When spices are well fried add the tomatoes. Mix with the fried spices and cook for 5 minutes. Add the water and let all come to the boil. Add salt and simmer for 10 minutes till gravy is thick. Add the burghers to the gravy just before serving and heat to let the gravy penetrate. Do not add the burghers too early or else all the gravy will be absorbed. Sprinkle with garam masala powder and coriander leaves before serving.

MUMMY'S MOWCHA CHENCHKI OR BANANA FLOWER CURRY

1-2 tblsp. oil

1 banana flower cleaned, boiled, and shredded small

1-2 green chillis deseeded and chopped

1 bay leaf

1 tsp. each coriander and cumin powder freshly roasted and ground

Salt to taste

Method

Heat oil, add bay leaf. When it begins to splutter add the mowcha and the spices. Fry all stirring continuously. Add the green chilli and salt and keep cooking till done. This is a good dry vegetarian dish with rice and dal and may be eaten with another curry item.

THORE CHENCHKI

(A '*Chenchki*' is a dry, basically lightly fried curry item without any added water. "*Thore*", for those who are not familiar with it, is the inner most section of the trunk of the banana plant. In Bengal one can buy it in the open market. I was always under the impression thore was eaten only by the Bengalis and was pleasantly surprised to learn it is also eaten in many of the Southeast Asian countries. However, they make it into a salad and use other oriental spices different from Bengal.

To clean the thore – cut in round slices. Now cut in thinner slices and if necessary, cut those in fours again. Apply plenty of oil to the palms. Take each round one at a time in the left hand. With the right hand pull the thread out of the thore in a twisting motion around the fore finger till all the thread comes off. Now cut them in thinner slices if necessary and cut those into fours again. Though this sounds difficult it is not so, once you've mastered the art. It is worth the effort and makes a delicious) vegetarian fare.

Salt as required	500 gm. thore cut small
1-2 tblsp. oil	1 tsp. whole mustard seeds
1-2 dry chillis	1 tsp. turmeric

Method

Rub salt into the thore and keep aside for ½ hr. or a little more. Before cooking press thore with both hands to let all the water out. Spread on a plate. Heat oil. Add mustard seeds and chillis. When they begin to splutter add the thore and turmeric and fry well till ready. This is a good accompaniment to an Indian meal along with lentils and other dishes.

Variation:

2or 3 potatoes cut very small could be added with the thore. For extra flavour also add 1-2 tsp raisins at this time.

THORE GHONTO

(*"ghonto"* is a dryish mushy curry item.)

500 gm. thore	3 tblsp. oil
1 tsp. whole cumin seeds	1 tblsp. ginger paste
2 tblsp. good rice	Salt to taste
1 tsp. coriander powder	1 tsp. turmeric powder
1 tsp. cumin powder	2-3 ripe tomatoes liquidized or, 2 tblsp. heaped tomato pureé or, 4 tblsp. yogurt
2-3 whole green chillis	1 tsp. garam masala powder
2-3 potatoes cut small	1 cup or less water
1 tsp. sugar	

Method

Treat the thore the same way as above and cut small. Heat oil and fry the rice and then keep aside. Heat oil, add more if needed and add the cumin seeds. When they begin to splutter add all the ground and powdered spices, (except garam masala), tomatoes or yoghurt, sugar, salt and chillis Fry all well. Add the thore, potatoes and rice and enough water to cover and cook. Cook till ready. It should be mushy with no liquid. Sprinkle with garam masala powder before taking off the heat.

SPINACH WITH BORI

(Boris are sun dried balls of various shapes and sizes made with different lentil pastes. These can be made at home but are readily available in all Indian grocery stores. The Bengali bori is different from the North Indian varieties which are spicier.)

6-8 red lentil boris	2 tblsp. oil
½ tsp. whole white cumin	2 medium potatoes washed, peeled, and cubed
2 medium brinjals cut in chunks	500 gm. spinach washed and chopped
Salt to taste	½ tsp. sugar
1 tsp. each cumin, coriander, and turmeric powder	1 tsp. pure ghee
1 tsp. 'garam masala' powder	1-2 green chillis (optional)

Method

Fry 'boris' in 1 tblsp. oil. Drain on paper towel and keep aside. Heat the rest of the oil and add whole cumin seeds. When the seeds begin to splutter add the potatoes and brinjal. Fry till potatoes are evenly golden. Add the chopped spinach and fry some more. Add salt, sugar, cumin, coriander, and turmeric powders and stir well. Add the ghee and continue to stir and fry the mixture. Add very little water only if necessary. Chilli may be added now. This vegetable dish should be mushy and well cooked. Add 'garam masala' powder, stir once and take off heat. Break up the fried 'boris' into tiny granules and sprinkle over the vegetable and serve.

SAAG PANEER

1 kg. spinach

1 tblsp. gram flour (*besan*) or plain white flour

2 medium tomatoes chopped

2 medium onions finely sliced

1-2 green chillis (optional)

A pinch of sodium bicarbonate

2 tblsp. oil

Salt to taste

Cottage cheese 300 gm.

Method

Boil or steam spinach with a pinch of sodium bicarbonate to get the bitterness of the spinach out. When cool liquidize spinach with gram flour. The gram flour is added to ensure the water in the spinach does not separate. Heat oil. Fry onions golden and then add the chopped tomatoes. Fry a little till well blended with the onions. Now add the spinach and cool for a little while till mushy, and the raw smell of gram flour disappears. Add salt according to taste and green chillis. Spinach is naturally salty so be careful when adding salt.

Fry the cottage cheese cut in cubes or rounds a golden-brown colour. Drain on paper towel. Add to the spinach during the last few minutes of cooking. Mix well till cheese is well coated with spinach. Don't overcook or cheese will crumble and the dish may become too dry.

NB   *Sag Meat* may be made in a similar manner. See "**Curries Non-Vegetarian**"

Variations

Suggestions for cooking the meat: Heat 2 tblsp. oil. Add 1 whole deseeded dry red chilli and 1 bay leaf. When they start to splutter, add and fry 1 medium sliced onion golden. Now mix the following in a bowl and add to the sliced onions: - 2 tblsp ground onion, 2 tsp ground ginger and garlic each, 1 tsp. each powdered turmeric, coriander and cumin.

Fry the spices well adding 2 tblsp. yogurt or 2 medium chopped tomatoes. When a nice aroma from the spices emanates, add the meat and fry well. Add just enough warm water to cook the meat. Dry off excess liquid before adding to the spinach.

When sag meat is ready sprinkle ½ tsp. powdered *garam masala* powder (pre-dry- roasted on a griddle), on top and serve.

KOCHUSAAKER GHONTO – CURRIED TARO (*Lat. Colocasia*) GREENS

500 gm. 'kochusaak' stems only, chopped very small

½ tsp. whole black cumin seeds

1 tsp. turmeric powder

Salt to taste

2-3 tblsp. oil

200 gm. shrimps or 4 heaped tblsp. fresh grated coconut

1 tsp. coriander powder

A pinch of sugar

1-2 fresh green chillis split

1 tsp. ginger paste

Method

Make sure only the stems of the greens are used. The leaves should be discarded. Boil the chopped stems after washing well several times under a running cold water tap. After boiling drain all the water out through a colander pressing down well. The vegetable must be completely dry with no trace of water as it is extremely sticky and acidic

Heat oil. Put in the cumin seeds. When they begin to splutter, add the vegetable with all the other ingredients and either shrimps or coconut. Keep cooking on low heat stirring frequently until dry and mushy. This dish takes a while to be ready and should be cooked slowly. Serve with rice and *dal* (lentils) as a vegetable accompaniment.

SORSE SAG (MUSTARD GREEN) CURRY

1 kg. or 2 large bunches of tender mustard greens cut small

3-4 fat cloves of garlic split

6-8 red ripe tomatoes chopped

1 tblsp. white mustard paste

Chilli powder to taste (optional)

1 tblsp. oil

1 tsp. whole black cumin seeds

2 tblsp. onion paste

1 tblsp. flour and water paste

Salt to taste

2 tblsp. butter

Method

Boil the chopped mustard greens. Throw away the water. Heat oil and add the black cumin seeds. When they begin to splutter add the greens with the garlic, onion and tomatoes. Mix and fry well. Add the flour paste and stir to mix. Now add the mustard paste and cook a few minutes longer till all well blended. Add salt and chilli powder. Cook a little longer. When done take off heat and cool. Put in the blender or food processor to purée. It should have a mushy consistency. Before serving, mix in the butter. Serve as a side vegetable with any Indian meal.

METHISAAK (FENUGREEK GREENS) FRY

2-4 tblsp. oil

1 medium long eggplant diced

2 large bunches *methisaak* chopped roughly

1 tsp. turmeric powder

1-2 green chillis (optional)

1 large potato diced small

½ tsp. black cumin seeds

½ tsp. cumin powder

Salt to taste

Method

Heat oil and fry the potato golden brown. Pick up with a slotted spoon and keep aside. Next fry the eggplant till red. Pick up with a slotted spoon and keep aside. In the same oil put in the black cumin seeds. When they begin to splutter add the *methisaak* along with all the other ingredients. Stir to mix and then cover. After a couple of minutes add the potato and eggplant and continue stirring. The water from the greens should dry off. When the vegetables are done take off heat and serve as a vegetable accompaniment with any Indian meal.

CHHOLA OR WHOLE BROWN PEA CURRY

1 cup whole brown chickpeas or, 'chola'

1 tblsp. oil

1 tsp. minced fresh ginger

1 medium tomato chopped

Water for cooking

2 medium potatoes cubed

¼ tsp. whole black mustard seeds

1 tsp. each of cumin and coriander powder

Salt to taste

Method

Soak peas overnight for several hours before boiling. Also boil the potato cubes. Heat oil. Fry mustard seeds. When they start to splutter add the ginger, cumin coriander and tomatoes. Mix well. Add the potatoes and peas and enough water to cook. Add salt. Gravy should be thick and mushy.

CHANNA OR DRY CHICKPEA CURRY (I)

250 gm. chickpeas	¼ tsp. bicarbonate of soda
2 tblsp. of oil	2 tblsp. onion paste
2 tsp. ginger paste	2 tsp. garlic paste
1 tsp. coriander powder	1 tsp. cumin powder
¼ tsp. cinnamon powder	¼ tsp. clove powder
¼ tsp. cardamom powder	½ tsp. chilli powder (optional)
2 medium tomatoes roughly chopped	Salt to taste
1 tsp. readymade tamarind paste or lime juice according to taste	Chopped fresh coriander leaves for garnishing

Method

Soak chickpeas overnight. Next day boil with the bicarbonate of soda (this makes the chickpea softer). Heat oil and fry all the ground pastes except tamarind. Next add all the dry powders and fry some more. Add the tomatoes and fry all together thoroughly. When the tomatoes and the spices are well fried and blended add the chickpeas soft and cook well. When almost done add the tamarind paste and a little water. This dish should be dry so, let all the excess water evaporates. If during the cooking process more water is required use the water in which the chickpeas were boiled. When ready sprinkle with chopped coriander leaves minus the hard stems.

DRY CHICKPEA CURRY (II)

250 gm. chickpeas	2 tblsp. oil
2 large onions sliced	1 tsp. thinly sliced fresh ginger
2 medium tomatoes cut lengthwise in quarters or eighths	1-2 tblsp. lime juice or, tamarind juice or paste
Salt to taste	2 tsp. heaped coriander powder
2 tsp. heaped cumin powder	½ tsp. paprika
Fresh coriander leaves for garnish	2-3 whole deseeded green chillis

Method

Treat and cook chickpeas as the above recipe. Heat oil. Fry chickpeas lightly on low heat. Add the onion and ginger slices and lightly toss till coated with oil and well mixed with the chickpeas. Now add the tomatoes and proceed the same way tossing gently to make sure the tomatoes do not become too mushy. They should be hard and yet coated with oil. The chillis could be added with the tomatoes or used later for garnishing. Dry roast the coriander and cumin powders. Next add paprika and salt.

Add to the chickpeas and toss gently to coat well. Take off heat and add the juice. Garnish with coriander leaves minus the hard stems.

This dish tastes better at room temperature – not too hot and not too cold. It makes a good teatime snack or as an accompaniment to a main course or an extra salad at the buffet table. This may also be referred to as" ghugni".

Variations:

1. The onions and tomatoes may be added raw after the chickpea has been fried but before adding the dry spices.
2. Small cubes of pre-boiled and fried potatoes (1 large) and chicken or mutton (100 gm.) may also be added at the same time as the chickpeas.
3. For extra flavour add 1 tsp. *'chaat masala'* available at all grocery stores.

PAKHI'S RAJMA

1 cup red kidney beans (*rajmas*) soaked overnight or, for several hours

1 tsp. turmeric powder

2-3 fresh green chillis

½ tsp. each cumin and coriander powder

Salt to taste

4 onions chopped

½" piece ginger minced

2 tblsp. oil

½ tsp. Kashmiri *mirchi* (chilli) for colour

Method

Wash the beans thoroughly and then pressure cook with 2 onions, ginger, turmeric, salt and chillis for about ½ hour or till beans are done. Heat oil and fry the remaining onions. Add the cumin and coriander powders and the colour. Stir for a few mins and then pour over the *rajma*. Serve with any Indian bread along with vegetable and or meat curry of choice.

SAMBHAR (WITH READY-MIX POWDER)

1 cup Arhar or Urad dal

1 tsp. turmeric powder

1½ tsp. ready mix *sambar* powder

Salt to taste

2-3 cups water

2-3 whole green chillis

1-2 tblsp. tamarind water (ready mix) or 2-3 tomatoes

Vegetable for Sambhar – The following combinations are recommended

(1) 3-4 potatoes quartered, and 2 large onions quartered

(2) 3-4 okras, 1 medium aubergine, 2 drumsticks cut in medium sized bits

(3) 1 small cauliflower separated into florets, 2-3 medium carrots quartered, a small handful of peas

There are many other combinations according to taste. However, it is not advisable to mix winter and summer vegetables in the same sambhar,

Method

Cook dal with water. Keep aside. Cook vegetables with just enough water to cover. Add turmeric, chillis and salt to taste. When vegetables are done add tamarind water or tomatoes. Cook another 5 minutes. Add cooked dal and sambhar powder. Let cook for 5 minutes. Add the following seasoning. Stir, remove, and serve garnished with a sprinkling of coriander leaves.

Seasoning:

1 tsp. oil or ghee

1 dry red chilli

1 tsp. whole black mustard seeds

A few fresh curry leaves

Heat oil. Add the above ingredients. When spluttering stops add to the hot sambhar on the stove and let it all mix well – about 1-2 minutes.

SAMBHAR (WITH HOME-MADE MIX POWDER)

1 tsp. oil
1 tsp. whole coriander
1 tsp. split chick-pea
2 tsp. grated coconut

1 small piece of asafœtida (not powder)
A pinch whole fenugreek
A few fresh curry leaves
1 tsp. chilli powder

(Powdered asafœtida may be used in which case it should be added just before the mixture is taken off the heat. However, for a better flavour, it is advisable to use whole asafœtida.)

Method

In a small heavy bottomed pan heat oil, add asafœtida. When it floats up add fenugreek, chickpeas, curry leaves and coconut, and chilli powder if using. Fry till all are brown and the aroma of sambhar starts to emanate. Put aside to cool. Grind to a smooth paste. Now it is ready for use. Serves 4.

Make sambhar according to the previous recipe substituting the above for ready mix. Sambhar made with home-made mix definitely adds a freshness to the flavour and the aroma is out of this world.

RASAM

1 cup arhar or urad dal	2-3 cups water
4-5 tomatoes or, 2 tblsp. tamarind juice	1 tsp. turmeric powder
Chilli powder and salt to taste	A generous pinch of asafœtida (optional)
1 tsp. rasam powder (ready-made or home-made mix.	1-2 tblsp. fresh lime juice

Method

Cook dal with water like sambhar. Squeeze the dal out and keep the water aside. To the water add the tomato or tamarind juice. Next add the turmeric, chilli powder and salt. Bring all to the boil. If using asafœtida add it now. Simmer for another 10-15 minutes. Add Rasam powder and cook another 5 mins. Add the seasoning like sambhar. Garnish with coriander leaves. Just before serving add a little fresh lime juice for taste.

RASAM WITH READY-MIX POWDER

1 tsp. oil

1 large pinch whole fenugreek

1 or 2 whole dry red chilli or 1 tsp. chilli powder

1 tsp. whole coriander

1 small piece asafœtida

Method

In a small heavy bottomed pan fry the above like sambhar. Cool and grind. If Rasam Powder needs to be stored, then dry fry all ingredients without any oil. Cool, grind and store in a jar with a tight lid.

BENGALI CHOLAR DAL (BENGAL GRAM) (I)

500 gm. cholar dal	Salt to taste
1-2 green chillis	2 bay leaves
2 tblsp. oil or good ghee	½ tsp. whole cumin seeds
1-2 red dry chillis de-seeded	2 tsp. ground ginger
½ tsp. turmeric powder	4 tblsp. grated coconut
¼ tsp. powdered mixture of *'garam masala'* (cloves, cardamom, cinnamon)	A pinch sugar

Method

Boil dal with sufficient water till done. Add salt, green chillis and 1 bay leaf and cook 1-2 minutes more. Keep aside. In another pan heat 1 tblsp. ghee to smoking. Add cumin, red chillis and bay leaf. Next add the ginger paste and coconut. Add the dal carefully and bring all to a boil. Add the rest of the ghee, 'garam masala' and sugar and more salt if necessary. Stir well, take off heat and serve.

BENGALI CHOLAR DAL (BENGAL GRAM) (II)

500 gm. cholar dal	Salt to taste
1 tsp. turmeric	1-2 cups warm water
1-2 tblsp. ghee	1-2 dry red chilli
2 bay leaves	4-6 cloves
3-4 split green cardamoms	1" piece cinnamon
2 tblsp. sliced onion	1 tblsp. sliced ginger
4-5 cloves garlic split in half	2 tblsp. grated coconut (optional)
1-2 tblsp. shrimps fried (optional)	A pinch sugar (optional)
1-2 fresh green chilli (optional)	100 gm. small cauliflower florets (optional).
	(Any other vegetables or chicken/mutton may be added)

Method

Cook dal with salt and turmeric. A little before dal is cooked heat ghee in another pan and fry red chilli, bay leaf, cloves, cardamom, cinnamon, sliced onion, ginger and garlic. If using coconut and shrimps this is the time to put them in. Add to hot dal and cook some more. Add sugar and more salt if necessary. Fresh green chillis split and deseeded may be added now for flavour.

If adding vegetables, it is better to half cook them and then add to the dal during the last minute of cooking. Do not add the water used to boil the vegetables in the dal.

Variation: If a lighter coloured dal is required use less turmeric. When dal is ready, cool and stir in a little bit of milk (1-2 tblsp).

SIMPLE BENGALI MOONG (YELLOW) DAL

250 gm. split yellow moong dal

Salt to taste

¼ tsp. whole white cumin

1 dry red chilli de-seeded (optional)

1-2 split and de-seeded green chilli (optional)

Water as required

2 tblsp. oil

1 tsp. thinly sliced ginger

A pinch sugar

Method

Wash dal well, cover with water and boil. Add salt and simmer on low heat. In the meantime, heat oil and add cumin seeds, ginger slices, and red chilli. When the seeds begin to splutter add it to the dal. Add salt, sugar and green chillis. Stir well and cook for another 2-3 mins. Take off heat and serve.

Variations:

'*Bhaja*' or fried moong dal – In this case dry fry or roast the yellow dal evenly in a skillet. Proceed as above.

PAKHI'S BLACK MOONG -- THE PUNJABI STYLE

1 cup black *moong* lentil (*dal*) washed well

1 tsp. turmeric powder

2-3 fresh green chillis

¼ cup fresh milk

¼ tsp. Kashmiri *mirchi* (chilli) for colour

2-3 onions sliced

½" piece ginger thinly sliced

Salt to taste

2-4 fresh cream slightly beaten (optional)

1-2 tsp. good ghee or oil

Method

Pressure-cook the dal with the onions, ginger, turmeric, salt and chillis for about ½ hour or till almost done. When cool add the milk and cook uncovered till dal is thick. When ready add the cream if using, stir gently and pour into serving bowl. Heat ghee or oil slightly and add the colour. Pour over the dal in the bowl. Serve with chapattis or any other Indian bread along with any vegetable or meat curry.

SWEET and SOUR ARHAR (TOOR GRAM) DAL

250 gm. arhar dal	2-3 cups water
1 tblsp. heaped jaggery grated or mashed	1 tsp. turmeric powder
2 tblsp. pitted dates well mashed	1-2 tblsp. tamarind juice or lemon juice
2 tsp. sliced ginger	¼ tsp. whole cumin seeds
¼ tsp. whole mustard seeds	¼ tsp. whole fenugreek seeds
1 red dry chilli (optional)	2 tblsp. oil or, clarified butter (ghee)

Method

Cook dal with water, jaggery, turmeric, dates. Make sure the jaggery and the dates are well blended with the dal. The dal should be soft but whole and not mushy. Add the tamarind or lemon juice and cook for another 2 minutes. Take off heat. In another fry pan heat the oil or clarified butter. Add all the other spices. When they start to splutter add to the dal and cook the whole for another 2-3 minutes. Serve with rice. This is a very cooling dish during the summer.

Variations

Can add thinly sliced green mangoes instead of the tamarind or lemon juice If a smoother dal is required add 2-3 tblsp. green mango pulp instead of slices.

GUJARATI ARHAR (TOOR GRAM) DAL

1 cup arhar dal cleaned and washed

1 tsp. turmeric powder

½ tsp. ground ginger

1 tblsp. oil or clarified butter

¼ tsp. black mustard seeds

¼ tsp. brown asafœtida

2 cups water or more

Salt to taste

1-2 de-seeded green chilli whole or minced (optional)

¼ tsp. fenugreek seeds

Method

Cook the lentils (dal) with water till soft. Add turmeric, salt, ginger, and chilli. Cook for another 5 minutes. In another pan heat the oil. Add the rest of the ingredients. When the seeds begin to splutter add the dal. Cook for another 2-3 minutes. Serve with rice or any Indian bread with any additional vegetable curry.

SOUPS

STOCK

(This is the basis of most soups and sauces.)

Mutton/chicken/beef bones or leftovers	Leek/onion/shallots
Carrots	Bouquet Garni (a mixture of bay leaf and dried or fresh thyme, and any other herbs as available)
Other herbs as available	

Method

Remove meat from bones. Chop bones in sizable pieces – remove fat and marrow and discard. Place bones in a saucepan and add cold water. Bring to boil. Remove scum gently. Add any leftover cooked meat. Lower heat and simmer for as long as possible. If necessary, add more cold water. Add vegetable and herbs and keep simmering for ½ - 1 hour. Keep on simmering and remove the scum from time to time. When ready strain.

In the days gone by a part of stock would be kept near the flame which would be simmering continuously. Cooks would keep adding bits and pieces of meat, vegetable peals to enrich the stock — called the boiling pot.

Variations

1. Fish stock can be made from bones, heads, tails of fish. Add to it herbs of your choice, onions, carrots etc.
2. Game stock — bones and leftovers, herbs as above, flavourings of choice.
3. Brown stock — brown bones or left over bones from a roast, water and herbs, flavourings as above.
4. Besides the above, stocks can be made with bouillon cubes.
5. Vegetable stock — different types of vegetables — carrots, peas, fresh beans etc. and their peels. Water, herbs, spices etc.
6. Worcester sauce, tabasco sauce, or any other commercial sauces of your choice may be added for an enhanced flavour.
7. Bones from chicken, mutton, beef, or pork after being boiled once for stock, can be refrigerated and re-boiled 2- 3 times for more added stock.

VEGETABLE SOUP

5 cups water

½ cup mushroom chopped

1 small, minced onion

4 oz. fine Chinese noodles (preferably rice noodles)

¼ cup peas

2 carrots grated

Salt and pepper to taste

Soy sauce and Tabasco to taste

Method

Boil all together except noodles, then simmer till vegetable done. Add noodles last of all. Add soy sauce and Tabasco for taste. Can also add bouillon cube. (If using soy sauce and bouillon cube, cut down salt). Add any other vegetable of choice or as substitute.

MINESTRONE

3-4 carrots	6 medium potatoes
4 oz. French beans	2 tblsp. butter/margarine
2 medium onions	1 bunch parsley
5 leeks	4 medium stalks celery
5 cups water	1 chicken/beef/vegetable bouillon cube.
2 tblsp. tomato purée	Ketchup (optional)
Salt and pepper to taste	2 fat cloves of garlic
8 oz. cut macaroni	Grated cheese of choice (e.g., parmesan, mozzarella, cheddar)

Method

Cut vegetable small. Melt butter/margarine in a saucepan. Add onion, parsley, leek, celery. Brown. Add the rest of the vegetables and fry a little. Add water and let boil till vegetables are done. Put in bouillon cube, tomato puree, ketchup, salt, pepper to taste. Simmer 15 minutes. Boil macaroni and add to soup just before serving. While still hot add grated parmesan, cheddar, or mozzarella to each bowl. Also serve a separate bowl of grated cheese for those with a cheesy palate!

BORSCH or BEETROOT SOUP (I)

4 cups stock/water	4 vegetable/chicken/beef bouillon cubes
2 cups shredded beet root	1 large, minced onion
1-2 tblsp lemon juice or red vinegar	Salt and pepper to taste
½ cup sour cream or beaten yogurt	

Method

Pressure-cook all above ingredients for 5 minutes except sour cream/yogurt. Cool. Put through blender or food processor reserving a little shredded beet. Add more water if necessary. Bring to boil. Simmer for 5 minutes. Serve hot or cold. In bowl put a little shredded beet. Ladle soup over it. Top with 1 heaped tbsp. of sour cream/yogurt.

Variations

1. The vinegar/lime juice may be reduced according to taste
2. A dash of paprika could be sprinkled over the sour cream/yogurt for those with a "tangy tongue" besides giving the soup an attractive appearance.
3. For a thicker and richer soup add one cup of finely shredded cabbage. Do not blend with soup. Add it to the soup when boiling. Simmer till tender. 3 or 4 medium sized potatoes may also be added which should be blended with the other ingredients.
4. Canned beet or baby food maybe used instead of raw beet. In this case do not pressure cook. Mix with all the other ingredients, blend and then boil and simmer.
5. Bouillon cubes may be substituted by 4 cups canned or packet soup prepared according to directions.

(You can think up many more variations to vary or improve the flavour of this very popular soup served cold or hot)

COLD BEETROOT SOUP (II)

1 kg. beetroot – cleaned with a brush under running water.

½ cup lemon juice

Salt and pepper to taste

Water

2 tblsp. lemon rind

Yogurt

Method

Pressure-cook beet root. Reserve the water. Mash beetroot or put through a food processor. To the beetroot add enough water to make 6 cups. Add beetroot mash, lemon juice, lemon rind, salt and pepper. Boil all. Simmer for 5 minutes. Cool. Serve with a little beaten yogurt in each bowl.

BEETROOT SOUP (III)

2 large beetroots, cut small   2 large carrots, cut small

1 large onion chopped   1 tblsp. Margarine/butter

2 tblsp. Tomato purée   4 cups stock or bouillon

Salt and pepper to taste

Method

Pressure-cook first 3 ingredients. Next add rest of the ingredients. Bring to boil. Simmer 5 minutes. Cool. Blend. Serve with the following cream:

<u>Cream</u>: Beat 1 tblsp. whisked yogurt, 4 tbsp. milk, and ¼ tsp. lemon juice

<u>Garnish</u>: with thin slivers or grated beetroot on top of cream.

SPINACH SOUP (I)

2 Cups steamed or frozen spinach

Salt and pepper to taste

1 tblsp cornstarch

1 cup milk

4 cups stock – chicken, meat, veg. or any kind of bouillon cubes

½ cup cream

Croutons

Method

Pass spinach through blender or food processor. Add stock, seasoning and bring to boil. Simmer 10 minutes. Blend cornstarch with milk, add to soup. Stir once or twice. Serve garnished with cream. (In bowl put croutons, ladle soup over them. Serve immediately or croutons will get soggy. Croutons may also be served separately.)

Variations

1. Instead of cream put 1 tsp. butter or margarine in each bowl of soup.
2. For a slightly richer and tastier soup for a party add 1-2 tblsp. Butter or margarine to the stock when boiling. Serve garnished with cream and croutons.

SPINACH SOUP WITH CORIANDER (II)

1 tblsp. oil	4 medium onions chopped
6 cloves garlic chopped or 1 tblsp. garlic powder	4 medium potatoes grated
6 cups water	1 kg. spinach steamed and mashed or frozen
1 large bunch coriander leaves	1 cup yogurt or I cup milk or half of each
Paprika	Salt to taste

Method

In oil stir onions till it changes colour – must not brown. Add garlic, stir 1-2 minutes. Add potatoes, stir till colour changes but again not brown. Add spinach, water, and salt to taste, and cook till potatoes are done. Add milk or yogurt (beaten) and let simmer on low heat for 3-4 minutes. Just before taking off fire add coriander leaves reserving a few for garnishing. Cool soup. Blend. If liked hot, warm soup slightly. Serve with paprika sprinkled on top. Garnish with coriander leaves. This soup maybe had cold or warm as above.

Variation

Puree spinach. Add enough water to get a 'soupy' consistency. Dry roast or grind 1 tsp. each of coriander and cumin seeds. Add to soup and simmer 5 minutes.

COLD CUCUMBER SOUP (I)

6 medium cucumbers   4 tblsp. margarine or butter or 2 tblsp. oil

2 medium onions   4 cups stock/water or any flavour bouillon cubes or 2 cups milk and 2 cups cream

4 tblsp. flour

Peel, deseed, shred cucumber fine. Make white sauce with margarine/ butter/ oil, onions, flour, and stock/milk. Add cucumber and cook till done. Add more milk/water if necessary. Cool and then blend. Simmer for 10 minutes. Put in the refrigerator till required. Serve topped with cream. (A good soup to serve for summer lunch or dinner.)

COLD CUCUMBER SOUP (II)

1 tblsp. butter/margarine oil

1 tblsp. flour

500 gms. cucumber peeled and sliced

Lemon juice

1/3 pt. cream

6 spring onions

1 pt. white stock

Salt and pepper to taste

1 sprig each of mint and parsley – chopped

Method

Melt fat in saucepan (if using oil, warm it). Cook onion over low heat until colour changes. Stir in flour and stock. Let come to boil. Do not let flour get lumpy. Add cucumber. Simmer till tender. Put in blender when cool. Add seasoning and lemon juice to taste. Before serving add chopped mint and parsley. Garnish with thin wafer like slices of cucumber with a little bit of green peel left on and 1 tblsp. cream.

COLD CUCUMBER SOUP (III)

2 cups yogurt

1 tsp. sugar

1 tsp. mustard

Chilli powder to taste

2 large cucumbers shredded

1 tsp. salt

½ tsp. black pepper

Method

Mix all above ingredients. Put through food processor. Add some chilled water if soup is too thick. Add a dash of Worcester sauce. Check for seasoning. A dash of chilli sauce enhances the taste especially for those who prefer something a little more hot. A dash of soy sauce could also be added - you cannot go wrong!

Chill before serving

POTATO SOUP (I)

4 large potatoes

2 tblsp. margarine/butter or 1 tblsp. oil

3 cups stock (any flavour) or 3 bouillon cubes with 3 cups water

1-2 tblsp. chopped plain or smoked ham or bacon (optional)

Paprika or dry green chilli powder or a few coriander leaves for garnish

1 large onion

3 cups milk powder (low fat may be used)

Salt and paper to taste

2-3 tblsp. cream (optional)

Method

Pressure-cook potatoes. Mash or put in food-processor. Chop onion fine. In saucepan put fat, onion, and potatoes on low heat. Mix all well, cook stirring continuously without letting onions and potato brown. When colour of onion changes, add stock or water and bouillon cube. Continue stirring or if possible, use a whisk so that the soup does not get lumpy. Once the onion is cooked and the soup looks smooth add the milk powder and continue stirring or whisking on low heat till soup is well blended and smooth without any lumps. Add salt and pepper. If chopped ham or chopped bacon is being used, put it in the individual bowls and then ladle soup over it. Add cream just before serving. Salt and pepper to taste should be added before the milk powder. Garnish with sprinkle of paprika or a few coriander leaves chopped fine or just 1-2 whole leaves. Use your imagination - you are sure to come out with a whole lot of wonderful ideas!

Variations

1. Instead of milk powder regular or low-fat milk may be used. Add 3-4 tblsp. milk to the soup or use part water and part milk.
2. The cream maybe added with the soup as suggested in the main recipe or as a garnish or mixed in individual soup bowls. The cream could be regular or substitute cream.

POTATO, CHEESE, CAPSICUM SOUP (II)

2 tblsp. margarine or 1 tblsp. oil	1 large onion chopped fine
1 large potato cut small	1 medium capsicum (½ green and ½ red) and 1 small red pepper.
1 bay leaf	1 tblsp. powdered cumin
4 cloves garlic chopped fine	1 cup beaten yogurt
6 cups water and 2 bouillon cubes or 6 cups stock	Salt
Paprika	Cheese – mozzarella, feta, cottage etc.

Method

Melt margarine. Add onion till changes colour and is soft. Do not brown. Add potatoes, stir a few minutes. Add chopped capsicum and garlic. Stir 1-2 minutes. Add water, bouillon cubes, cumin, salt, bay leaf and paprika. Let come to boil. Lower heat. Simmer 15 minutes. Cool. Take out bay leaf. Blend soup. Strain if necessary. Once more put soup on low heat for 5-10 minutes. Add little water if necessary. Before serving add beaten yogurt and heat on low flame or microwave on warm. Put soup in bowls and while still warm add grated cheese so it melts. Can also pass around a bowl of extra cheese for those with a cheesy tongue/pallet!

TOMATO SOUP (I)

4 cups tomato juice	4 cups consommé, stock or equivalent made with bouillon cubes and water.
4 whole cloves.	8 peppercorns.
1 small bay leaf	1 tsp. chopped basil.
1 small onion chopped.	Salt, pepper to taste.
3 sprigs parsley.	Cream for garnish.
Lemon juice and Tabasco to taste.	

Method

Bring all to boil and simmer for 15 minutes. Strain. Serve hot or cold. Garnish with cream. If serving hot add croutons to individual bowls or serve separately.

TOMATO SOUP (II)

250 gms. ripe red tomatoes skinned and chopped

2 tblsp. flour

4-5 cups water or stock.

2 tblsp. margarine/butter

1" piece ginger minced fine or 1 tsp. ginger powder.

2-4 tblsp. tomato paste/purée

2 medium slices of bread made into croutons

1 tblsp. cream.

Salt pepper to taste.

Method

Puree tomatoes in blender. Keep aside. In a saucepan make a roux with the flour and margarine on low heat. Pour stock in gradually, stirring continuously. Soup must not get lumpy. When it comes to boil add tomato puree, ginger seasoning. Simmer 5 minutes. Serve in soup bowls topped with beaten cream and croutons.

The croutons maybe put in the soup bowl with the soup ladled over. However, if not consumed immediately they can get soggy. I prefer to serve them separately. (A little extra dash of freshly ground pepper and 1 tbsp. Worcester sauce gives the soup an extra tang.)

Variations

1. The above may be made with either canned tomatoes, packet or canned tomato soup, baby food or tomato puree - the latter, if used, should be mixed with water to bring it to the proper consistency. This can only be done by tasting as different brands of tomato puree have different strength and taste.

2. For even a quicker tomato soup put stock or water in saucepan with 2 or 3 bouillon cubes, 4 tbsp. ketchup, 2 tbsp. tomato puree, 1 tbsp. Worcester sauce, 1 tsp paprika. Bring all to boil and then simmer. Check for seasoning. Thicken with corn flour if necessary. When ready add 2 tsp. margarine (optional). Serve with cream on top. The corn flour and margarine can be made into a roux with a little of the stock (not milk) as the base of the soup, and then the rest of the stock and sauces could be added.

3. Canned tomato juice can also replace fresh tomatoes.

4. To the tomato pulp add tomato paste (for extra colour), bouillon cubes and water or stock. Let all come to boil. Add dry roasted powdered coriander, cumin (according to taste), turmeric, chilli powder (optional). Heat and simmer for 15 minutes. Add corn flour if soup is too thin.

5. Follow the method of the main recipe excluding the beaten cream and ginger. Dry roast 1-2 tsp. each of whole coriander and cumin. Cool and grind to powder. Mix with the soup and simmer 5-10 minutes. Serve sprinkled with a dash of paprika or chilli powder. Alternately, add the powder with the flour and margarine roux.

BASIL AND TOMATO SOUP

1 cup tomato peeled and chopped

½ cup fresh mushrooms chopped

1 green, red, or yellow pepper minced

¼ cup black olives chopped

½ tsp. dry oregano

Salt and freshly ground pepper to taste

1 cup fresh basil leaves washed and chopped

2-4 cups chicken stock

½ tsp. dried Italian seasoning

1 tblsp. corn flour for thickening

Method

Liquidize tomato, basil, mushroom, pepper, and olive in a blender till smooth. Mix the purée with the chicken stock and the rest of the ingredients except corn flour, in a saucepan and bring to the boil. Simmer covered for 15 minutes. Add the corn flour just before taking off the heat stirring well till blended, and soup begins to thicken. Can serve with *croutons*.

Variation

If preferred the mushrooms, olive and pepper need not be liquidized with the tomato and basil. These may be added when the soup is simmering. Equally delicious!

GREEN PEA SOUP

250 gm. fresh green peas pressure-cooked

2 tblsp. flour

2 bouillon cubes (optional)

4-5 cups of water

2 tblsp. margarine/butter

Salt and pepper to taste

¼ cup cream

Method

Purée peas in blender or food-processor. In saucepan make a roux with fat and flour on low heat. Pour stock or water gradually stirring continuously so that soup does not get lumpy. When all the stock/water has been poured add puree and bouillon cubes if using. Add seasoning. Simmer on low heat for 15-20 minutes. stirring frequently. Serve in individual bowls topped with cream.

Variations

1. Frozen peas may be used instead of fresh peas. These will not need pressure cooking. If necessary, soak in warm water and then puree. For added thickening, canned baby food may also be used which can be added to the soup without blending.

2. Instead of flour use corn flour/cornstarch. In that case no need to make the roux. Put all the ingredients together except butter/margarine in the saucepan and bring to boil. Simmer for 5 minutes. Now add the margarine/butter. Let it melt. Mix corn flour/cornstarch in ¼ cup milk. Add gradually to the soup. Keep stirring till well mixed, about 1 min., take off heat. Serve with cream.

CORN SOUP

½ cup whole corn kernels or 1 cup creamed corn

4-5 cups water or stock or a combination of bouillon and water

1 tblsp. soy sauce

2 tblsp. margarine

Salt, pepper, paprika to taste

2-4 tblsp. milk

2 tblsp. corn starch/corn flour

Method

Pressure-cook whole corn kernels if used. Next put the corn kernels/creamed corn in the blender or food processor. Use the water in which the corn has been pressure cooked. Make sure it comes out as a paste. Put all ingredients except milk and corn starch/flour. Bring to boil. Simmer for 10 minutes. on low heat. Now add the corn flour/starch diluted in cold milk. Stir for 1-2 minutes. Take off fire and serve hot with extra soy sauce and chilli or tabasco sauce separately. Put a few whole corn kernels in each soup bowl.

Variations

1. Like some of the previous soups, baby food or canned/packet corn soups may be used.
2. Whole corn on the cob could be used, in which case about 2-3 medium sized ones. After pressure-cooking take the kernels out and proceed as above.

BEAN SOUPS

These can be made with any kind of beans or lentils. They are filling, nourishing and delicious! Ideal for vegetarians. Children love them too as they can be a meal by themselves. All you need is a bit of imagination and a little experimenting. To the basic soup you can add some vegetables of your choice or ham, bacon chicken etc. Here are a few recipes for bean and lentil soups to set you off. You can add some or take away some – just have fun and enjoy! Bean and lentil soups taste better if they are thick. (To make life simpler suitable canned beans are available.)

BLACK BEAN SOUP

1 cup black beans

2 tblsp. margarine or butter.

1 stem celery

2 bouillon cubes

4-5 cups of water

Plain or smoked ham or bacon or, Chinese sausage (optional)

1" piece ginger

1 large onion

Salt, pepper to taste, cayenne, mustard

1 tblsp. Worcester sauce

2 tblsp. low fat powder milk

1 tblsp. sherry/brandy

Method

Soak beans for about 2 hours or overnight, if necessary. Pressure-cook with finely sliced ginger 15 minutes. Cool. Blend or put in a food processor.

In saucepan melt fat. Sauté finely chopped onion till changes colour. Add finely chopped celery. Stir a few minutes. Add processed beans. Cook a couple of minutes. Add all seasonings, bouillon cubes, sauce, and water. Bring to boil. Simmer on low heat 10-15 minutes. Cool, strain, blend, or process once more. Return to low heat for 5 minutes. If too thick add more water. Add powdered milk and stir gently. Now add chopped ham or bacon. Just before serving add the brandy or sherry. Garnish - A swirl of cream with a sprinkling of paprika.

Variations

1. 1 tblsp. celery salt/powder or dried celery can be used instead of fresh celery which should be added with the seasonings.
2. The chopped ham, bacon or sausage may be placed in individual bowls and the soup ladled over. Garnish as above.

RED BEAN SOUP

1 cup any red beans	1 tblsp. oil
1 bay leaf	2 large onions
1 tsp. cumin powder	1 tsp. coriander powder
½ tsp. turmeric	1 cup chopped tomatoes
½ cup tomato puree	1" piece ginger
4-5 cups water with 1-2 bouillon cubes/stock	Salt and pepper
Chilli powder to taste (optional)	3 tblsp. boiled rice (optional)

Garnish – coriander leaves, lemon slices.

Method

Soak, pressure-cook and process the red beans the same way as the black beans. Warm oil in saucepan. Add bay leaf. Next brown the onions golden. Now add cumin, coriander, and turmeric powders. Stir a few minutes. Add tomatoes and tomato puree and fry well till all well blended. Add the beans and finely chopped ginger. Cook a few minutes. Add water and bouillon cubes or stock. Let all come to boil.

Simmer on low heat for 10-15 mins. Add salt, pepper and chilli powder if using. When soup is ready, take-out bay leaf and discard. This may be served with 1 tblsp rice in each bowl with the soup ladled over. Garnish with a sprinkle of coriander leaves. Serve with slices of lemon.

SOYA BEAN SOUP

1 cup soya beans

2 bouillon cubes of any flavour (optional)

Salt pepper, cayenne to taste

2 tblsp. margarine

1 large onion chopped

4-5 cups water (if using powder milk increase water to 5-6 cups)

1 cup milk, or 4 tblsp. powder milk

Method

Soak, pressure-cook and process soya beans like in all other bean soups. In saucepan combine soya bean mash, onion, bouillon cubes and water and bring to boil. Simmer on gentle heat for 10 minutes. Add margarine, seasonings and milk which has been warmed slightly. Continue stirring so the milk does not curdle. Take off heat when soup reaches a fairly thick soup consistency. More water or milk may be added depending on the consistency required. (If using milk powder, no need to warm or dilute with water. Add the powder straight to the soup and continue stirring). Extra cream may be added, if desired, as garnish in the individual bowls.

BAKED BEAN SOUP

2 cups baked beans in tomato sauce (any brand or homemade)

1 bouillon cube – beef, chicken, or vegetable

1 medium capsicum minced

2 tblsp. fresh coriander leaves minced

4-6 cups water

Salt and pepper to taste

2 tblsp. butter (optional)

2 tblsp. cream or 2 tblsp. skimmed milk

1 bowl croutons served separately

Method

Bring all the above ingredients except butter and cream/milk to the boil. Simmer for 5 minutes on low heat covered. Cool. Put through the food processor or blender till smooth. Just before serving warm slightly, add the cream/milk and butter. Serve in individual bowls with the croutons.

Variations

1. If desired do not add the minced capsicum and fresh coriander leaves at the beginning. Add them only after the soup has been put through the food processor just before warming.

    However, there is a subtle flavour when all the ingredients have been cooked together and put through the blender. A few pieces of minced capsicum and coriander could be saved for garnishing.

2. Instead of croutons a bowl of plain boiled rice may also be served separately with the soup with slices of lime.

3. 2 tsp. curry powder could be added to the soup when boiling for added flavour.

LENTIL or *DAL* SOUP

1 cup lentil or any kind of dal	1-2 tblsp. oil
1 bay leaf	1-2 large onions
1 tsp. turmeric powder	1 tsp. cumin powder
¼ tsp. chilli powder (optional)	1 tsp. coriander powder
1" piece ginger	2 tblsp. tomato puree
¼ cup minced mutton/ chicken/ vegetables (peas, diced carrots, potatoes, cauliflower)	5 cups water
Salt and pepper to taste	1-2 bouillon cubes (optional)

To be served separately – slices or wedges of lime and boiled rice (optional)

Method

Boil or pressure-cook lentil/dal till soft. In a saucepan warm oil. Put in bay leaf. After 2 minutes add and fry chopped onions till golden brown. Add all the spice powders and chopped ginger. Continue stirring for two minutes. Add tomato puree and continue stirring another 2 minutes. till well mixed. Now add mutton/chicken/vegetables. Keep a handful aside for later use Cook 5 minutes. with sprinkling of water so that meat and spices do not stick to the bottom of the pan. Add warm water and bouillon cubes and bring to the boil. Lower heat and simmer for 15 minutes. Take out the bay leaf. Put soup in the blender. Fry one finely sliced onion deep brown. Add to the blended soup and put back on medium heat. Boil once. Serve in individual bowls. Make sure each bowl has some meat or vegetables and a few fried onions.

Pass around slices of lime and boiled rice separately.

Variations

1. For a plain dal soup omit the mutton/chicken/vegetables. Add bouillon and water after purée. Continue making the soup as given above. Serve with wedges of lime with or without the rice.
2. This soup can also be made with left over dal. Blend the dal mixture. Add bouillon cube(s), water according to taste and depending on the amount of left over dal. For extra flavour, add a little ketchup or Worcester sauce or any other sauce of your choice. Just keep experimenting and tasting to get the best flavour!

GREEN *MOONG (DAL)* SOUP (from leftovers)

½ -1 cup left over green moong (dal)

1 - 1½ pt. water

1 tsp. curry powder (optional)

1 tsp. freshly roasted and ground cumin

1 or 2 egg yolks

1 tblsp. ketchup or any other sauce (optional)

Salt and pepper to taste

Croutons or a little rice with lemon wedge

Method

Put the dal through a food-processor till smooth. Add egg yolk and sauce if using.

Process a little more till all well mixed and there are no lumps. Put mixture in a saucepan and add water. Add curry powder and seasoning. Bring soup to boil on high heat constantly churning with a hand rotary beater. Reduce heat and simmer for 10 minutes. Serve in soup bowls sprinkled with cumin powder and croutons immediately or pass the croutons separately. Any other left-over dal can be made into a soup with a little bit of imagination. Any left-over chicken or mutton curry added to it will give it that extra kick! You will have guests raving.

MULLIGATAWNY SOUP

2 tblsp. Oil	1 large bay leaf
2 large onions chopped	2 large onions liquidized
1" piece ginger liquidized	4 large cloves garlic liquidized
1 tsp. coriander powder	1 tsp cumin powder
1-2 tsp. turmeric powder (depending on the colour desired)	1-2 tblsp. Tomato purée
4-5 cups water or stock	2-3 bouillon cubes
1 cup minced chicken/mutton/vegetables (e.g. peas, bit pieces of carrots, potatoes, French beans etc.) – (optional)	1 tsp. chilli powder (optional)
A few curry or coriander leaves (optional)	

Method

Warm oil in pan. Put in bay leaf. After 2 minutes add chopped onions and brown. Next add all the liquidised and powdered spices and fry well for a few minutes. At this time add the curry or coriander leaves, if using. When the spices tend to stick to the bottom of the pan add the tomato puree and continue frying. Sprinkle water from time to time so that the spices do not burn and stick to the bottom of the pan. If using chicken/mutton/vegetables, now is the time to add those to the spices and continue frying. When all the solids and spices are well blended add the water/stock and bouillon cubes (optional if using stock). Bring all to boil a couple of times. Now lower heat and simmer till meat/vegetable are cooked and the mixture reaches a nice soupy texture. Before serving, take out the bay leaf, curry/coriander leaves and any other bold spices which have not blended with the soup. Make sure each individual bowl has some meat/vegetable. Serve with wedge of lemon and boiled rice separately.

Variations

This soup may be made with curry powder. In which case, use 2 tsp. curry powder instead cumin and coriander powder. If the curry powder being used is hot, use less or exclude the chilli powder according to taste. It is very important to make sure that this soup is well cooked so that there is no taste of raw spices.

CHICKEN AND CORN SOUP (I)

½ cup shredded chicken (preferably from the breast

½ cup corn kernels/creamed corn or 2 whole corns on the cob

4-5 cups chicken or corn stock or/and water and bouillon cubes

Salt, pepper, paprika to taste

2 tblsp. corn starch

1 tblsp. soy sauce

1 egg (optional) beaten

4 tblsp. milk

Method

Pressure-cook chicken and corn (if using whole or kernels) for 5 minutes. Cool and strain. Reserve a little chicken and corn. Blend the rest with a little of the stock. Boil mixture with the liquid from the pressure cooker and the stock just once. Simmer on low heat for 10 minutes. Add seasoning and soy sauce. Mix corn starch/flour with cold milk and gradually add to the soup. Take off heat. Put a little shredded chicken and corn that has been kept aside in each bowl and ladle soup on top. Serve with soy sauce and chilli sauce separately for those who would like to add some extra flavour. Can add 1 beaten egg by pouring it in a thin stream just before taking soup off heat. If egg is used reduce the corn starch to 1 tblsp.

CHICKEN AND CORN SOUP (II)

3 oz. margarine

1 tsp. powdered garam masala

1 tsp. salt

1/3 cup corn kernels

¼ cup nutmeg

10 cups water

Cayenne pepper to taste

2 sliced onions

2 tsp. ground garlic

1 cup large, sliced mushrooms

4-5 whole black pepper corns

8 oz. shredded chicken

1 cup cream

Garnish - 1 tblsp. fresh coriander leaves

Method

Melt fat on a low flame. Add onions and all spices, chicken, mushrooms, corn. Cook. Cool. Keep a handful aside which should be chopped fine or minced. Liquidise the rest. Add 10 oz. of water to the mixture. Bring to boil. Lower heat and simmer for 15 minutes. Before serving, put a little of the mince in each bowl and pour the soup on top. Add cream. Sprinkle coriander leaves and cayenne on top as garnishing.

CHINESE CHICKEN AND NOODLE SOUP (I)

5 cups chicken stock or, chicken bouillon cube stock

3 tblsp. Soya sauce

Black pepper to taste

6 oz. Chinese noodles

8 oz. shredded chicken

1 tsp. tabasco or chilli sauce

1 egg – well beaten

Method

Bring stock and chicken to boil. Simmer for 10 minutes or till chicken is done, if uncooked. Add noodles, soy sauce, chilli sauce, pepper and salt if required. Just before serving beat egg into soup in a thin thread before taking off heat. Serve with soy and chilli sauce ort Tabasco.

CHINESE CHICKEN AND NOODLE SOUP (II)

4 oz. shredded uncooked chicken

2 tblsp. soy sauce

2 tblsp. dry sherry

Salt, pepper to taste

2 oz. mushrooms (cut if too large)

4 cups chicken stock or water with two chicken bouillon cubes

8 oz. Chinese noodles

1 tblsp. chilli sauce or, sprinkling of tabasco sauce (optional)

2 tblsp. finely chopped spring onion

1 large whole egg, or 2 egg whites or 1 tblsp. egg powder as substitute

Method

Bring chicken and stock to boil. Add noodles, sauces, sherry (if using), seasoning, mushroom and finely chopped spring onions. Simmer till noodles are done. Just before serving, heat soup if necessary, and then pour well-beaten egg in a thin stream. The soup will immediately thicken, and the egg will resemble thin threads. Ladle into the bowls while still hot.

CHINESE CHICKEN AND VEGETABLE SOUP

1 large onion sliced

2 medium carrots – sliced thin lengthwise

4 oz. whole small or, sliced large mushrooms

5 cups chicken or bouillon cube stock

4 oz, shredded cooked chicken

2 tsp. light soy sauce

3-4 stems spring onions – cut ½" lengths

8-10 any large spinach leaves (*'pooi'* is the best)

Salt pepper to taste

Method
Boil all vegetables except spinach leaves, in stock once and then simmer till vegetable done. Add chicken, sauce, seasoning, spring onions and spinach leaves, and cook till all done. Serve with soy, tabasco, or chilli sauce.

Variations
If desired, a handful of rice cooked or, cooked noodles may be added at the last minute.

CHINESE SOUR AND HOT SOUP

1 tblsp. soy sauce

4 cups water or, any kind of stock

2-3 beaten eggs

½ tsp. black pepper

½ tsp. ajinomoto or sugar (optional)

Any bits of leftover meat – cut small and mixed with a little corn starch

2 tblsp. corn starch

2 tsp. salt

4 tblsp. vinegar (red) or wine

½ tsp. sherry

Mushrooms, spring onions, tofu etc. (not noodles) may be added

Method

Mix soy sauce, gourmet powder and corn starch with 1 cup cold stock. Bring to boil the remaining 3 cups stock. Add the 1 cup cold stock. Lower heat. Beat eggs in a small bowl and pour over soup very slowly, stirring constantly. Add vinegar, pepper, and anything else that is being used. Tofu to be added last, if used, as it may crumble.

CHAWAN MUSI (I)

('Chawan' means a bowl and 'musi' means steamed. Literally, steamed in a bowl. The soup can be served in individual serving bowls.)

2 eggs	A bowl of thick brown soup
3 cups bouillon soup	1-2 tsp. light soy sauce
Salt to taste	Mushrooms, cooked shrimps/chicken, spinach leaves

Method

First put the eggs into 8-10 cups of soup and then add 3 cups bouillon to the cooled soup. When bouillon is cooking, add soy sauce, salt to taste. In each cup place a few slivers of cut mushroom, boiled shrimps or chicken, boiled spinach leaves. Pour soup over it. Cover each bowl, keeping a little opening. Steam about 15 minutes. Though this is soup, it sets like a thick custard after steaming.

CHAWAN MUSI (II)

A little bit of tender chicken sprinkled with salt

Mushrooms, carrots

A piece of white fish sprinkled with salt

Salt to taste

1 tblsp sugar

4 eggs

Boiled spinach leaves

Shrimps

1 tblsp. soy sauce

2 tblsp. 'sake' or white wine

4 cups old stock

Method

Put all the above except stock and egg in a bowl.

Break eggs in a bowl. Stir well. Add to seasoned stock and stir again. Pour over rest of ingredients. Place bowl covered with foil in double boiler or, steamer or, over pan of hot water. Cook on low heat till it becomes like custard. Must not get too hot, otherwise it will become spongy.

SIMPLE JAPANESE SOUP

5-6 cups boiling water	1-2 bouillon cube (any flavour)
1 tblsp. soy sauce (preferably light Japanese)	Salt to taste
Bits of chicken	1 tblsp. white vinegar
5-6 large eggs depending on the number of persons (1 egg per person)	Mushrooms – 2 per bowl
Parsley for garnish	

Method

(Proportion ½ cup boiling water per person. 1 bouillon cube for 10 people and ¾ tsp. soy sauce per person).

In boiling water add bouillon cube, soy sauce and salt to taste. At this stage, taste soup for correct flavour.

Beat egg.

Take a small, rounded spoon, pick up egg in it. In a bowl put 3 parts boiling water add 2 tblsp. white vinegar. Put beaten egg through a sieve into the water. Remove from heat and strain to take out water. Pick up egg with small, rounded spoon and put in each soup bowl. Continue this way depending on the number of eggs used. (This is best done with one egg at time in ¾ part water and a dash of vinegar. It is more manageable.) Now take another 1-part boiling water with salt and cook bits of chicken for 5-10 minutes. Strain. Put 1 or 2 bits of chicken by the egg in the soup bowl. Put a couple of mushrooms in each bowl and a little chicken stock. Garnish with parsley.

SOUP WITH BUTTER DUMPLINGS

Dumplings

4 eggs – 8 egg whites as substitute may be used	2 tblsp. milk
Dash of ground cloves	1 tblsp. parsley – chopped fine
Salt pepper to taste	2 tblsp. margarine/butter/shortening/oil
Breadcrumbs	Dash of nutmeg

4-6 cups of soup made from mutton/chicken/vegetable stock or bouillon cubes

Method

Beat egg, milk, spices well. Add parsley and seasoning. Fry onion and shortening till soft and very lightly brown. Add enough breadcrumbs to the eggs to make it a little thick. Cool fried onions and then add to egg mix or else it will curdle. Add more breadcrumbs, if necessary, to make into balls. Wait 5 minutes after adding breadcrumbs before making the balls. If too thick, add a little more milk. Be careful not to add too many breadcrumbs. Otherwise, dumplings would become very 'bready' and hard. Drop balls into boiling soup. Simmer 10 minutes. (Wet hands before making balls). Serves 4.

PRAWN SOUP

250 gm. Prawn heads	1 tblsp. oil
2 medium onions	1 tblsp. flour
2-2½ cup prawn stock and water	1 bouillon cube
2 oz. cheddar or mozzarella sliced or grated	1 tsp. Worcestershire sauce or, ½ tsp. anchovy or fish sauce
2 tblsp. ketchup	1 tblsp. butter
Salt and pepper to taste	1 tblsp. cream

Method

Fry prawn heads in very little oil till crispy. Grind and then pressure-cook in a cup of water. Cool and strain through soup strainer. Fry chopped onions in the rest of the oil golden brown. Add flour and fry some more stirring all the time. Add prawn stock and water, bouillon cube, ketchup, sauces used and seasoning. Bring to boil on high heat and then simmer 15 minutes on low heat. Add cheese in the last minute of cooking. Take off heat and add the butter and cream or only one of them.

HUNGARIAN GOULASH SOUP

Noodles:

1 cup flour   1 egg

Pinch of salt   Water

Soup:

4 tblsp. fat/oil   4 large onions sliced

1 kg. beef/mutton/chicken cubed   500 gm. potatoes

1 heaped tsp. paprika   1 green pepper chopped

1-2 carrots chopped   1 small celery chopped

4-8 cups or more water

Method

Heat oil. Fry onion till golden. Add meat and continue frying (lower heat if necessary) till brown. Do not let onions brown – remove, if necessary, till meat is done. Return onions to pan. Add paprika and stir to mix. Add water, potatoes, all vegetables and cook till three quarters done.

For the noodles, mix all with just enough water to make a stiff dough. Take off bits and drop in the soup while meat and vegetables are cooking.

Remove when all well-cooked. Add more water if necessary. This dish is specially appetizing on a cold wintry day. Eaten with chunks of fresh Italian or French bread you will be more than satisfied

----

YAHNELI KUFTE (Armenian)

1½ kg. leg of mutton (lean)

Salt, black pepper to taste

½ tsp. allspice

3 cups *borghol* washed well

Dash of chilli powder

Method

Mince mutton fine – best done in food-processor. Take out fat, if any. Mix with *borghol* and all other ingredients above. Once more put in the food processor till smooth. Form into large balls. To hold the filling comfortably, make a depression with the thumb. Put in filling, seal, and make into ball again. Small ball may be made without any filling. Both together can be put in the soup.

Filling

2 tblsp. butter/margarine or 1 tbsp. oil

1-2 tblsp. minced chicken/soya chunk (original recipe requires sheep's fat, sheep's tail or any other fat, suet etc.)

Large pinch of allspice

3-4 medium onions – finely minced

Black, red or soya beans

Melt butter/margarine. Fry finely minced onions. Add minced chicken or soy chunk and a large pinch of allspice. Mix well. The chicken/soy grains or beans should be minced fine in the food processor.

Soup

3 eggs (or substitute

1 litre yogurt

Salt to taste

4 cups mutton stock

A little cooked, chopped mutton

Beat eggs, add stock little at a time to eggs and continue beating till half the stock is used up. Then add remainder of stock with the chopped mutton, all at once. Beat yogurt and add egg stock mixture a little at a time and keep beating till all is used up. Put on low heat and keep stirring — do not let it curdle. Gradually bring to boil. Put in meat balls and simmer 15 minutes. Add seasoning.

Melt 2 tbsp. butter/margarine or level tbsp. oil. Add 1 heaped tbsp. dry mint powder. Let mix. Take off heat. Put in soup and serve.

P.S. Dry mint in sun or in oven, crush to powder. Store in dry place.

MIDDLE EASTERN CHICKEN and RICE SOUP

6 cups chicken stock or, made with bouillon cube (any flavour)

2 eggs (or, egg substitute)

Salt and pepper to taste

¾ cup uncooked shredded chicken preferably from shoulder

½ cup rice

2 tsp. lemon juice or, ½ tsp. lemon powder

Method

Cook rice with seasoning in stock. When ready, strain stock and keep in reserve. Beat eggs or substitute with salt and pepper and pour in a thin stream on very hot rice stirring with a wooden spoon continuously. Add lemon juice and mix well. If using lemon powder mix it with the egg and then add to rice. Now bring chicken shreds with stock to boil. Next simmer till chicken is done — approx. 2 minutes. Serve the hot rice separately with the soup or, add 1-2 tblsp. or more of rice to each serving bowl of soup.

MIDDLE EASTERN MUTTON SOUP

2 cups chopped mutton (breast, shoulder, or neck)

A few soup bones

6 cups water

1-2" cinnamon

2 oz. Capellini/very fine noodles or thin vermicelli

Salt and pepper to taste

Parsley for garnish

Vegetables: all or some suitable substitute may be used -- 4 oz peeled or chopped tomatoes, 1 stick celery – chopped, 3 small finely sliced carrots, 1 small, cubed squash

Method

Pressure-cook meat and bone with sufficient water till done. When cool, skim and discard all fat if any. Now add vegetable, cinnamon, seasoning after discarding bones. Bring to boil. Add noodles and then simmer till vegetables cooked. Serve sprinkled with chopped parsley.

HODGE PODGE SOUP

Method

A very interesting soup which does not need much imagination but can be very tasty and even be served as a party fare. In the basic stock (if you have any ready), put in any leftovers e.g. casseroles, cottage pie, lentil, vegetable curries etc. etc. (there is no end to it). Add herbs or any other spices or sauces if you have the inclination to do so. Add more water if necessary. Stir. Whisk. Simmer. Cool when ready. Blend well. Strain. Warm again. Serve with whatever garnish you fancy.

Variations
1. If no stock available use bouillon cubes and water.
2. You can make meat, chicken, fish, or vegetable soup this way

Note

Often, we have several types of leftovers of very small quantities. These can be awkward for serving. What can be a better way than combining several leftovers, adding a bit of this and a bit of that and, turning out a delicious first course i.e. "SOUP"!

(However, be careful in combining the various leftovers — they should complement and not contradict each other e.g. fish curry and mutton pie or, a bit of left over dessert!

THICK BROTH

Method

Another soup with leftovers! This can be made with any leftover dish such as meat or chicken stew, steak, and kidney pie (this is especially good), cottage or shepherd pies, vegetables etc. Mash all or put it through the food processor which is preferable to get a smooth soup like texture. Put in a saucepan with the required amount of water, seasoning, sauces if used, and bring to boil on high heat. Lower heat and simmer for 10 minutes. A good wholesome yet light supper dish. Serve with Toast and cheese. (If using a bottled sauce for the extra flavour I recommend either a steak or hamburger sauce, A-1 sauce, Dippy's Sauce or any other similar substitute.)

COLD YOGURT SOUP

(This is a refreshing starter for a hot summer day or night. Yogurt soup can be served before either an Indian menu or a mixed buffet.)

2 cups yogurt (not too sour)	1 cup chicken/mutton/vegetable stock or, 1 cup water with 2 bouillon cubes – vegetable or chicken or mutton
1 tsp. roasted ground cumin powder	1 tblsp. lemon juice
1 tsp. roasted ground coriander powder	Salt to taste
½ cup cream (optional) or, butter milk	Pinch of cayenne or red pepper
Finely chopped fresh mint or coriander leaves	¼ tsp. black pepper

Method

Beat yogurt till smooth. Add stock (non-fat) gradually. Mix well. Mix all other ingredients except cream. Last of all add the lightly beaten cream and stir. There should be no lumps in the soup. Serve in soup bowls. Garnish each bowl with a sprinkling of black and red pepper and a mint or coriander leaf in the centre. This soup should be chilled before serving for the best flavour.

VARIATIONS OF COLD AND HOT SOUPS

1 can of condensed chicken or beef soup diluted with ½ can water. To this add the water from any canned vegetable e.g. beetroot, carrot, peas, corm, asparagus, mushrooms etc. etc. Always check for salt before adding as the water from canned vegetables is normally salty. Heat and then cool if serving cold. Add 1-2 tblsp. milk or top of milk or cream. 1 tblsp. butter (optional) and a dash of freshly ground pepper and paprika, if desired. Serve hot or cold.

BREADS AND ROLLS

QUICK EASY WHITE BREAD

(2 Loaves – 1 lb. each)

1 tsp. level dry yeast

A little warm milk or water to soak yeast

1 tsp. salt

3 oz. margarine

1 tsp. sugar

2 lb. flour sifted

1 pt. milk

Method

Mix yeast, sugar, and warm water or, milk and rest for a few minutes till bubbles appear. If using milk it can be taken from the warmed pint of milk. Sieve the flour and salt together. Warm milk and margarine together. If too hot, keep aside to cool to warm or tepid. Pour milk mixture into yeast mixture. Now pour all into flour mixture. Mix well. Cover with a tea towel or cheese cloth and leave to rise in a fairly warm place but not hot – e.g. a cool oven. Let dough rise to double its size. This should be no problem, provided the yeast is not dead, during the hot weather but the rains and cold weather could delay the process of rising.

Place the dough on a floured board and knead well adding more flour, a little at a time, as needed till dough is smooth and all stickiness disappears. Do not make it too dry. (This can also be done in a food processor with success in which event the manual labour is reduced!). Now place dough in 2 greased but not floured 1lb bread tins to rise uncovered. Dough should cover the top of the tin. Immediately put bread in the middle shelf of a pre-heated moderate oven or Gas Regulo Mark No:6. Baking time approximately 1 hour. When loaves are ready and still hot brush tops with cold milk. Take out of oven and turn over to cool on a wire tray. Gently ease out the loaf tins.

Variation:

For a healthy brown bread replace white flour with whole-wheat flour (*atta*) – the coarser the better. Instead of 1 tsp. white sugar use 1 tsp. brown sugar. Continue with the same process as the white bread.

BACHELOR'S or STUDENTS' EASY BREAD

10 tblsp. level crystal sugar

14 oz. white flour

1 tsp. clove powder

5 oz. almonds or, any other nuts peeled and thinly sliced.

3 eggs

2 tsp. baking powder

2 tsp. cinnamon powder

5 tblsp. honey warmed

Method

Beat sugar and egg till smooth. Mix all the dry ingredients and add to the egg mixture stirring gently. Add the honey and stir till all well blended. Grease and flour a 1 lb. loaf tin generously. Pour in the batter and smoothen the top. Bake in a medium oven for 30-40 minutes. Check for doneness by inserting a toothpick in the middle which should come out clean. Slice and serve warm with butter, jam, or soft cheese.

BREAD ROLLS

(15 Rolls)

1 tsp. level dry yeast

A little warm water or milk

1 tsp. salt

1½ oz. margarine

1 tsp. level sugar

12 oz. flour sifted

½ pt. milk

Method

Proceed as above "Quick and easy bread". Then take off bits from dough and shape as required. Put on greased baking sheet and let rise a little till shape looks good. (If left to rise too much the rolls will spread and not come out well. Another alternative is to put them in individual roll tins or deep cupcake/muffin tins if a round shape is required. Let the dough in this case come up to the top of the tins.). The rolls should take approximately ½ hour in the middle shelf of a moderately hot oven or Gas Regulo Mark–6. When rolls are ready and while still hot brush them with milk to get a shine. Cool on a wire tray.

BEIGLI (SESAME ROLL)

Dough:

2 tsp. dried yeast	4 tblsp. sugar
½ cup lukewarm milk	500 gm. flour
4 tblsp. margarine	1 tsp. baking powder
2 eggs	1 tsp. grated lemon or, orange rind

Filling:

15 tblsp. black sesame seeds	2-3 tblsp. raisins
2-3 tsp. milk for a soft consistency	1 tsp. sherry or cognac for flavouring
1 tblsp. powdered sugar	
1-2 eggs for brushing pastry	

Method

Mix the ingredients for the filling and divide into 3 portions. Keep aside till required.

In a small bowl mix the yeast, 1 tblsp. sugar and 2 tblsp. lukewarm milk. Let rise to double. In another bowl sift flour and baking powder. Rub in the margarine till resembles breadcrumbs. Add the yeast mixture. Add the eggs one at a time, stirring with a wooden spoon after each addition. Next add the grated rind, the rest of the sugar and milk to get a soft dough. If required a little more milk may be added. Leave to rise for ½ to 1 hour. Divide dough into 3. Roll each fairly thin (should be easy to handle) and spread with 1/3 of the filling. Now roll each like a Swiss roll and leave to rise. Place on a greased baking tray. Brush with a little egg yolk. Rest for a little while. Again, brush with egg yolk and rest. Once again brush with egg yolk. Prick top with a fork and bake in moderate oven for about 1 hour. When cool sprinkle with powdered sugar, cut in slices and serve. Fresh cream is an additional accompaniment as a party fair!

ICE BOX OR REFRIGERATOR ROLLS

½ cup water

¼ cup sugar

3 cups plain flour

½ cup butter

1 tblsp. dry yeast dissolved in ½ cup water

Method

Heat water, butter, and sugar till the sugar dissolves. Cool. Combine all the ingredients except the flour. Last of all beat in the flour gradually a little at a time. Use the dough attachment if using an electric hand beater. Continue beating until the dough becomes a satiny texture. Wrap and cover dough in a bowl with greased wax paper. Keep in the refrigerator till required. Can be kept this way for 3-4 days. When required take out and place dough on a floured board pressing down flat. Cut in ¼"diameter rounds and place on a baking tray. Cover with a floured cloth and let rise for about 1 hour. Bake in a moderately hot oven for about 10 minutes.

The rolls can be cut into any shape and size as required. They can also be cut into triangles and rolled up like croissants.

HOT ROLLS

2 tsp. yeast	2 tblsp. lukewarm water
1 cup milk	1 cup butter/margarine
3 eggs slightly beaten	5 tblsp. sugar
4½-5 cups (or more) flour	1½ tsp. salt

Method

Add the yeast to the lukewarm water. Heat the milk to boiling point but do not let it boil. Take off heat and cool to warm. Add the butter while milk is still hot. When milk is cool gradually add the beaten eggs, sugar, and the yeast. Sift flour and salt together and add to the milk mixture. If necessary, add more flour to get the right consistency. Put dough on a lightly floured board and knead until smooth – approximately 5 minutes. Brush top of dough with melted butter or oil to prevent a crust from forming. Cover with a cloth and place in a warm place (e.g. a closed cool oven) to double in size. Punch down and shape into rolls. Place in an oiled baking sheet/tray. Turn rolls over to coat with oil all over to get an even brown. Let the rolls rise 3 times the original size. Bake in a hot oven for about 15–20 minutes. When ready, brush tops with butter while still hot to give the rolls a nice gloss. This should make 3 dozen rolls of any shape – round, plaits, twists, croissants etc.

Variations:

Sweet Rolls – Shape the rolls into little balls. Dip in melted butter and roll in any kind of crushed nuts. In a ring pan place the rolls one on top of each other halfway up the tin, leaving a little space between each roll. Bake as above. When ready take out of the oven and let rest for a few minutes. Put a plate over the ring tin and turn over to get the rolls out. Serve the rolls attached to each other. Each person should pull the rolls out with their fingers according to their needs.

Note. In a high altitude use 2 tblsp yeast and 4 tblsp lukewarm water. Also, after the first rising of the dough punch it down and turn over and let it rise a second time before shaping into the desired shapes.

SIMPLE BREAD ROLLS/STICKS AND PIZZA DOUGH

1 tsp. heaped dry yeast

2 tblsp. lukewarm water

½ tsp. salt

2 eggs

1 tsp. sugar

8 oz. flour

2 tblsp. butter or, margarine

¼ cup milk (more or less) if required

Method

Mix the yeast with the sugar in the warm water and leave in a warm place covered till bubbles appear. In the meantime, sift the flour with the salt. Add the butter and mix till like breadcrumbs. Next add the eggs one at a time and mix well. Make a well in the centre of the dough and add the yeast. Gradually draw the flour from the sides into the yeast and mix till all well blended. Add just enough milk, if necessary, to form a smooth dough. Cover and leave in a warm place to rise. Knead well and cover once again and let rise. Shape into bread rolls, bread sticks or for a large or small pizza/s. Leave to rest and rise double, for the rolls and sticks and sufficiently for the pizza/s. Bake in a hot oven for ½ hour to 45 minutes or till done.

METHI PARATHA

2 cups flour

2 tblsp. oil

Water for mixing

Extra oil for frying as required

1 tsp. salt

1 cup fresh/dry *methi* (fenugreek) leaves washed and chopped

Method

Sieve flour and salt together. Add oil and mix till resembles breadcrumbs. Add the *methi* leaves and mix well. Add enough water to make a soft pliable dough. Make small balls the size of a squash or table tennis ball, flatten with rolling pin and roll out the size of *parathas* (5" diameter) or the size of a saucer. Brush surface of griddle or non-stick pan lightly with oil and cook *parathas* one by one. When small bubbles appear on one side carefully turn over and cook the other side till done on medium heat. Serve with vegetarian or non-vegetarian curry or just plain yoghurt and cucumber salad.

Variations:

1. Make parathas as above using green or red spinach instead of fenugreek leaves. Only use the leaves minus stems.
2. Coriander, mint, basil leaves can be substituted for *methi* leaves.
3. In the absence of fresh leaves use dried *methi*, coriander, mint, or basil leaves in which case, mix with the flour and salt before adding oil.

BAKING POWDER PARATHAS

2 cups flour

1 tsp. baking powder

5 tblsp. heaped ghee or oil

Oil or melted ghee as required

1 tsp. salt

1-2 eggs

2-3 tblsp. or more yogurt

Method

Sift flour salt and baking powder. Add the eggs one by one, mix and then gradually add 2 tblsp melted ghee or oil and mix all well. Add yoghurt as required to bind the dough which must be pliable – not too dry and not too sticky. Knead well, cover, and leave to rise in a warm place for 1-2 hours. Punch down and form 12 balls. Roll out in rounds the size of a quarter-plate. Heat a griddle and lay a *paratha* on it. When bubbles appear take ½ tsp. ghee or oil and slip it around and under the *paratha*. When slightly cooked and bubbles appear on top turn *paratha* and slip another ½ tsp ghee or oil around and under it. Now keep turning the *paratha* several times so that it doesn't get burnt on one side. Do not add any more ghee. Gently poke the centre to verify doneness. Take off heat and serve immediately or store in a warm place till required. Make the rest of the *parathas* this way.

These *parathas* resemble something in between a *naan* and a *tandoori roti* and are soft and delicious. A good accompaniment with kebabs of any type.

EASY PARATHAS

Method

Any of the above parathas or stuffed parathas can be made with bread, pizza, or any yeast dough. They can also be rolled small and fried like puris. However, it is advisable to cook the parathas or fry the puris as soon as they are rolled out because of the yeast dough. These parathas and puris should be eaten as soon as they are made. They do not store well and when cold develop a rubbery consistency.

EGG PARATHAS

4 cups flour	1 tsp. baking powder
½ tsp. salt	1 tblsp. ghee or, oil
4 tblsp. yogurt	1-2 tblsp. water for mixing, if required
Additional melted ghee/oil for frying	

Topping:

¼ tsp. salt	2 eggs well beaten
3 small onions chopped	6-8 green chillis de-seeded and chopped
3-4 tblsp. melted ghee/oil	1 large bunch fresh coriander leaves chopped fine

Method

Sift flour, baking powder, salt. Add ghee/oil and yogurt. Mix and knead dough thoroughly, adding water only if required to bind and form a smooth and pliable dough. Let it rest covered in a warm place. Knead lightly once more and form into 12-13 balls. Roll each ball thin on a floured board, the size of a saucer. Heat a griddle and place a *paratha* on it. Slip ½ tsp melted ghee/oil under it. Keep turning the *paratha* with a spatula in a circular movement. Do not turn the *paratha* right over. Mix the salt and the beaten egg. Spread 2 tsp of the egg on top of the *paratha*. Sprinkle ¼ tsp each of onion, chillis and coriander leaves on top of the egg. Top the mixture with a sprinkling of another ½ tsp melted ghee/oil. Make sure the mixture adheres to the paratha by pressing down and continuously turning round with a spatula. When the egg sets, turn the paratha over, shifting it around constantly. When the paratha turns a golden brown remove from griddle and keep in a warm place. Continue with the rest of the parathas in the same way. These can be served with '*aloo dum*', or any other vegetarian or non-vegetarian curry with a yoghurt-based salad or *raita*.

TANDOORI ROTI

500 gm. white flour

1 tsp. dry yeast or, 1 oz. (scant) fresh yeast

Salt to taste

Warm milk for mixing

½ tsp. baking powder

1 tsp. sugar

1 tblsp. ghee melted or, oil

¼ tsp. bicarbonate of soda

Method

Mix together flour, baking powder, yeast, sugar, salt and the bicarbonate of soda. Add melted ghee and mix. Next add sufficient milk a little at a time to make a pliable dough. Knead well, cover, and leave in a warm place to rise. When dough rises to double its size, add the bi-carbonate of soda diluted in very little milk and mix well – make sure it is well blended and doesn't adhere to only one side. Knead a little more if necessary. Take off bits and roll the size of *chapattis* or a saucer. Place a *roti* on a griddle. Dampen top of roti with water. Put the griddle with dampened roti on the Bar-B-Q. When one side is done turn the griddle on the open fire. The roti will rise and get detached from the griddle. Rub roti with melted ghee, if desired, and serve immediately or store in a warm flask till required. Better not to make too much in advance.

If a Bar-B-Q is not handy then place the roti on top of the fire of a gas cooking range making sure to dampen the top. When done, toss over and place under the grill. When it rises and is done rub with melted ghee as above and serve. This is an equally good way of making tandoori roti though the smoky taste will be absent.

GUJARATI MUSLIM CHAPATTIS

1 cup flour

4 tsp. oil

1-2 tblsp. wheat flour (*atta*)

Salt to taste

Water for mixing dough

Method

Sift flour and salt. Add 2 tsp oil and mix. Next add sufficient water gradually to make a soft pliable dough. The dough should not be too dry or too sticky. Knead well and then take bits of dough and make into small balls. Roll out the balls flat resembling small coasters or *puris*. Press the centre of each with a little oil and sprinkle the top with *atta*. Draw up the sides of each and again roll into balls. Now once more roll out the balls flat into very thin *chapattis*. Place *chapattis* one at a time on a hot griddle and keep pushing it from side to side so it does not get burnt and all the sides get cooked evenly. Turn over quickly and push it around. Turn once more and press down gently with a fish slice so that it puffs up. Take off heat and press *chapatti* down with hands or tea towel. This will keep it soft and prevent it from becoming dry.

PEA KOCHURI

Dough:

2 cups flour

1 tblsp. oil or, ghee

½ tsp. salt

½ cup (or less) cold water for mixing

Filling:

1 tsp. oil

1-2 tsp. ginger paste

½ tsp. asafœtida powder

Oil for frying *kochuris*

1-1½ cup frozen or, fresh green peas boiled and mashed into a paste

1 tsp. cumin dry roasted and ground

Method

Sift flour and salt on a board or table. Make a depression in the centre. Pour the oil into the depression. Draw the flour gradually to the centre and keep mixing with the oil till resembles breadcrumbs. Add water a little at a time and keep mixing and kneading till a soft pliable dough is formed. Should not be too dry or too moist and sticky. Form the dough into a ball.

Knead for a couple more minutes, cover with a bowl and keep aside till filling is ready.

Heat oil in a pan. fry the green pea paste with the asafœtida and ginger juice till well mixed and raw smell disappears. Take off heat and sprinkle cumin powder and mix.

Make very small balls (the size of a large marble) from the dough. Roll like *puris*. Place 1-2 tsp. filling in the centre and draw up the dough from all sides to cover it. Tap lightly with the rolling pin and gently roll flat and round but not too thin. Brush a non-stick frying pan or, skillet, and fry the *kochuris*. With a teaspoon put very little oil around the *kochuris* in the pan but not directly on them. Fry a light brown. Then turn over and repeat the processes. The *kochuris* will puff up.

Serve hot with *chutney* or, '*aloo dum*'. A good dish to serve for lunch/dinner or as a snack for tea/drinks.

If a richer *kochuri* is desired, deep fry them.

RICE

COCONUT RICE

2 cups rice

1 large onion sliced and lightly fried golden

1 tblsp. oil

3 cups or more coconut milk

Salt to taste

Method

Clean and wash rice several times under running water. Drain off all water and spread on a tray. Leave for 10-15 minutes. Place the rice on a heavy bottomed saucepan. Cover with coconut milk. it should come 1" above the rice. Add salt, onion, and oil. Mix well and cook like plain rice till all water has evaporated. Delicious served with any chicken curry.

Variations:
1. The onion may be added without frying
2. Substitute 1" sliced ginger or, ½ tsp. ginger powder instead of onion slices.

JAPANESE RICE

(This is best cooked in a pressure cooker)

5½ cups small grain rice

2 tblsp. soy sauce (optional)

1 tsp *ajinomoto*

¼ cup mushrooms thinly sliced

5½ cups very hot chicken stock

1 tsp. salt or, to taste

¼ cup chicken cut into cubes

¼ cup green string beans cut thinly on the slant

Method

Wash rice well and then place in a pressure cooker. Add the stock and all the other ingredients. (The soy sauce adds colour and flavour. Use Japanese or a light soy sauce). Close pressure cooker and cook on high heat for 10-25 minutes or till pressure is reached. Reduce heat to low and cook for another 5 minutes. Remove from heat. Open the lid only when the pressure has gone down. Rice may be left in the pressure cooker without opening the lid till required. Serve in a bowl or flat dish.

Variations:

1. Instead of chicken stock add boiling water in the following proportions – to each cup of rice add 1 and 1/10th cup of water.
2. Place thinly shredded cabbage on individual plates. Top with fresh or cooked thick narrow beef fillet cut in slices. Cover with cooked rice. The fillet could be roasted, fried or steamed with seasoning and soy sauce

----

QUICK RISOTTO

1 tblsp. olive oil	1 large or, 2 small bay leaves
3-4 whole garlic	500 gm. ground meat (beef or lamb)
2 medium onions chopped	1 bouillon cube (beef or chicken)
2-4 tblsp. tomato purée	2 cups water
1 cup long grain rice	1 cup green peas
1 medium red pepper seeded and shredded	1 bunch spring onions chopped
1 tblsp. oregano/Italian seasoning/mixed herb	1 large carrot diced (optional)
Salt, pepper and paprika to taste	¼ cup or more grated parmesan cheese or substitute.

Method

Heat oil slightly in a saucepan. Add the bay leaf and the whole garlic. Stir for a couple of minutes. Add ground meat and onion. Cook stirring from time to time till the colour of meat and onion changes. Add crumbled bouillon cube, tomato purée and the water. When the water comes to the boil add the rice, half cover and cook. When the rice is almost cooked add the green peas, pepper, spring onions and the herbs. At this time add the carrots also, if using. Stir adding more water if required. Add the seasonings. When rice and vegetables are done, and the water dried up take off heat. This dish should not be too mushy. Constant stirring during cooking is a must. Serve sprinkled with grated cheese along with a bowl of extra cheese for those who may require more. If parmesan is not readily available cheddar or any other medium flavoured cheese can be used.

Note:

Left over risotto pie

If risotto is left over, place it in a heat - proof dish. Cover top with creamy mashed potato seasoned with any herb of choice (e.g. parsley, cilantro, mint etc.) and salt, pepper and paprika (optional). Stick bits of bread cut in small triangles on the potato. Alternately sprinkle the mash potato with breadcrumbs and then grated cheese. Bake in a moderate hot oven till top is browned or microwave. This dish can also be just browned under the grill. Serve with a green /tomato salad.

SIMPLE GUJARATI PULAO

1 cup rice	1 tblsp. oil or, ghee
1 bay leaf	3 cloves
2 green cardamoms whole	1" piece cinnamon
½ tsp. whole cumin	1 carrot cut small
2 potatoes quartered small (optional)	½ cup small cauliflower florets
2 tblsp. green peas	1 tsp. turmeric powder, if a yellow pulao required
Salt to taste	

Method

Heat oil or, ghee. Add all spices except turmeric. When they begin to splutter, add all the vegetables and fry. Add turmeric and salt. When vegetables are well fried add the rice and fry another 3-4 minutes stirring continuously. Add enough water to cook the *pulao* – ½" above the rice. Add more later only if necessary. This *pulao* should not be soggy. Each grain of rice should be soft and stand out separately.

GUJARATI KITCHRI

1 cup rice	1 cup *dal* (lentil) – *moong, arhar* (*toor gram*) or any other kind
½ tsp. whole cumin	½" fresh green ginger thinly sliced
1 bay leaf	3-4 whole cloves of garlic
1" piece cinnamon	Salt to taste
1 tsp. turmeric	A large pinch ground asafœtida
½ tsp. chilli powder	2 tblsp. ghee

Method

Put all the above ingredients in a large saucepan with enough water to come ½" above all the ingredients. Let all come to boil. Cover and cook till done stirring from time to time. Add more water if necessary.

Variations:

1. If a slightly richer *kitchri* is required, then just boil the rice, dal, salt, turmeric, and water to come ½" above the ingredients. if necessary, add more water. Let all come to boil and then cook covered, stirring from time to time until done. Remove from heat. In another pan heat the ghee and add all the rest of the spices. When they start to splutter add to the *kitchri* and place on heat to cook for another 2-3 minutes.
2. Instead of using half rice and half dal you can substitute ¾ rice and ¼ dal.

KHITCHRI THE PARSI WAY

1 tblsp. ghee/butter/margarine/oil	1 small onion chopped finely
½" piece cinnamon stick	2 small cardamoms
2 cloves	1 oz. '*masur dal*' (red lentils) cleaned, washed, and soaked for ½ hour
8 oz. rice cleaned, washed, and drained	¼ tsp. turmeric powder
1½-2 cups hot water	Salt to taste

Method

Heat the cooking medium used and fry the onion till light brown. Add all the other ingredients except rice, salt, and water. Keep frying by stirring continuously for about 5 minutes. Add the rice and continue stirring till it begins to stick to the pan. Add salt and hot water which should be about 1" above the level of the rice. Bring to the boil and then simmer on very low heat till rice and lentils are cooked. Serve hot with Fish *Sas* or Chicken/Mutton curry and a salad or '*raita*' of choice.

Note: 12 oz. rice per person is a generous measurement if only the above accompaniments are served.

BORA BIRIANI

1 kg. mutton cut in large serving pieces OR, 1 large chicken (approx. 1½ kg.) cut in large serving pieces

1 tsp. each cumin, coriander, and turmeric powder	2 tsp. each ginger and garlic paste
6 tblsp. ghee (butter oil)	¼ tsp. chilli powder (optional)
2" piece cinnamon	½ tsp. whole cumin seeds
6-8 whole black pepper	4-6 cloves
1 kg. half-boiled and cooled rice	Salt to taste
¼ cup raisins	5-6 medium potatoes peeled and cut in half
1 medium banana leaf well washed	4-6 medium onions peeled and cut in half
3-4 cups unsweetened yogurt unbeaten	2 tsp. saffron soaked and softened in 1 tblsp. warm water.
1 burning (smouldering) charcoal	

Method

Cook meat with the powdered spices and ground pastes, with just enough water to cover for ½ hour. Alternately pressure cook for approximately 5-7 minutes. When done dry off the excess water on top of the stove. Keep aside. In a small wok or fry pan heat 2 tblsp ghee. Add the whole spices. When they begin to splutter add to the meat and cook for another 2-3 minutes. Now add the salt to taste.

Line a big saucepan with 3 tblsp melted ghee. Lay a thick layer of rice on the ghee. Cover rice with a layer of meat. Now add a layer of potatoes, onions. Next, add a sprinkle of raisins, saffron and yogurt. Keep repeating the layers minus the ghee. The top layer must be rice.

Sprinkle the charcoal with 1tblsp melted ghee. Wrap charcoal well in the banana leaf securely. With a pair of tongs insert the package into the biriani from the centre. This is the secret of the biriani which gives it a smoky flavour. Cover dish with a secure tight-fitting lid, sealing the edges with a thick paste of flour and water. Cook on low heat very slowly till the potatoes etc are done, and the liquid if any has evaporated and the biriani aroma hits your nose. The biriani should not be mushy. The rice grains should be fluffy but moist – not too dry.

Serve with a <u>Cucumber *Raita*</u>: 2 cups well beaten unsweetened yoghurt. 1 medium cucumber grated or cut in thin shreds. 1 tsp sugar. 2 tsp salt. ½ tsp undiluted mustard powder. 1 green chilli deseeded and chopped. Mix all. Refrigerate before serving. May garnish with a sprinkle of paprika and chopped coriander leaves.

To vary the '*raita*' add 1-2 medium tomatoes chopped. The quantity of the above spices for the raita may be varied according to taste. Can also add a sprinkle of cumin powder with the above garnish.

FISH BIRYANI

(For this recipe, fish with less bones and a little on the fatty but tasty side is preferable. Prawns with the heads and tails cut off are also a good substitute. Fish suggested are from the carp family - rohu, bekti or snapper, blue fish etc. etc.)

1 kg. basmati rice	4-6 tblsp. oil
4 large potatoes cut in quarters	4 large onions thinly sliced
4-6 cloves	A large pinch of saffron
2 cups (or more) beaten unsweetened yogurt	4-6 cardamoms
2 bay leaves	1 tsp. cumin powder
2 tsp. garlic paste	500 gm. fish cut in large serving pieces
2 tsp. turmeric powder	4 tsp. onion paste
2 tsp. ginger paste	1 tsp. coriander powder
4-5 whole allspice	4 tblsp. pure ghee or butter melted
1½ cup frozen peas	4 hardboiled eggs sliced or quartered
1 tblsp. rose or 'kewra' essence (optional)	

Method

Wash the rice well and then spread out on a large tray. Next half cook the rice and keep aside. Fry the onions a dark brown, drain on paper towels and keep aside. Fry the potatoes a golden brown and keep aside.

Add saffron, cloves and cardamoms to the beaten yogurt and keep aside. Smear the fish pieces with the turmeric and salt and let rest for about 15 mins. Heat the rest of the oil in a deep fry pan. Put in the bay leaves. After 1 min add all the pastes and powders and fry well sprinkling a little water from time to time to prevent the spices from sticking to the pan. When there is no longer the raw smell of spices, add the fish and fry gently without breaking them, with the spices. Once the fish is done add the salt and enough water to reach 1" above the fish. Let it come to a boil, then cover and cook for another 10-15 minutes or less.

Take a large flat-bottomed saucepan. Spread 2 tblsp melted butter at the bottom. Line with a thick layer of rice. Place a few pieces of fish with some gravy over the rice. Top with some potatoes, peas, eggs, and fried onions. Sprinkle a generous amount of curd to cover all. Repeat the process till all the ingredients are finished. The bottom and top must be rice. Sprinkle the rest of the ghee on top of the rice. Sprinkle rose/kewra essence on top. Cover tightly and cook on low heat till done. This can also be cooked in a slow oven. However, the taste and aroma is more appetizing when cooked on top of the stove. Turn out onto a flat serving dish and gently mix the ingredients. Garnish with a little fried onions and eggs. Final garnish can be done with silver foil.

GLOSSARY

Ajinomoto	Monosodium glutamate (MSG)
Aloo	Potato
Aubergine	Brinjal or egg plant
Ahrar dal	Yellow lentil. Also known as 'tuvar'
Au gratin	A dish quoted with sauce, sprinkled with cheese and crumbs browned in oven or under grill
Barfi, burfi	Dry and sugary Indian confectionary
Bati-charchari	Another type of dry Bengali curry
Beorek	A Middle Eastern pastry dish
Bhapa	Steamed Indian food
Brinjal	Eggplant or aubergine
Bhujia	Dry fried or oven roasted mixed savoury nuts, lentils etc.
Biryani (Biriani)	A special type of 'pilau' usually cooked with meat
Borgul	Cracked wheat
Bori	Shaped and sun-dried balls or lumps of lentils
Casserole	Slow cooked food in a covered heat-proof dish in oven or the utensil itself for such
Chanchra	Bengali dry curry of assorted vegetables
Chapatti	Or roti, handmade, usually round, flat unleavened bread
Charchari	Dry Bengali vegetarian curry
Channa	Cottage cheese similar to 'paneer'

Chenchki	Another type of Bengali dry vegetarian curry
Chop suey	"Mixed spice" in Chinese – an American dish of meat (chicken, beef, pork, prawn) cooked quickly with vegetables
Cholar dal	Lentil made out of split brown peas
Crepe	Word of French origin, fine pancake
Curry powder	A mixture of various Indian spices often used for making curries (commercially available)
Daab	Green coconut
Dal	Any Indian lentil usually with the specific type mentioned before e.g., moong dal
Dalia	Broken wheat used as porridge and in various other dishes
Dalna	Bengali curry with gravy
Dárazsfeszek	Sweet pastry of Hungarian origin
Doi	Yogurt
Dolma	Stuffed vegetable
Dum	Vegetable normally cooked under pressure
Eggplant	Aubergine, brinjal
Escalopes	Flattened meat or fish
Falafel	A Middle Eastern snack
Fettucine	A type of Italian flat pasta
Flambé	A dish, sprinkled with spirit, set alight before serving
Flan	An open tart filled with fruit, cream, custard etc
Galantine	French dish with meat or poultry served cold covered with aspic

Ghonto	A 'mushy' Bengali vegetarian (sometimes non vegetarian) curried dish
Granola	Cereal mixture made of many nutritious items
Gulab jamun	A very popular fried Indian sweet in syrup, brown in colour
Hilsa	Very popular migratory ocean fish caught in the rivers of Bengal delta, akin to 'shad' of the Americas
Hulwa	Also known as Hulva. Soft Indian sweet
Jackfruit	A tropical fruit eaten raw when ripe or cooked while green as a vegetable.
Jhaal	A Bengali curry with chilli hot gravy. Also, peppery or chilli hot
Jhole	Bengali stew
Kalia	A rich and spicy Bengali curry
Kalo Jam	Indian black berry growing in a large tree, supposed to have medicinal properties
Khasta	Indian flaky pastry
Kheer	Indian milk dessert
Kitchri	A mixed rice and lentil preparation
Kochuri	Indian snack of wheat casing and vegetable, lentil (sometimes meat) stuffing usually fried in round shapes
Kofta	Ground meat, fish, or vegetable ball
Korma	A type of rich meat/fish/vegetable curry
Langosh	Or 'Langosch; Hungarian savoury cake
Lo-mien	Chinese dish with noodles, vegetables, meat, shrimps, seafood, and wontons.

Ma	My mother-in-law, Nilima Ghosh, who had a small repertoire of some very tasty dishes.
Malai	Cream of milk
Malpoa	Bengali fried sweet pancake in syrup
Methi	Fenugreek
Meringue	Small pâtisserie made from egg white and sugar
Mishti	Bengali sweets in general
Moong	A green lentil
Moussaka	A meat and egg-plant preparation of Greek origin
Mousse	A cold souffle
Mowcha	Flower of banana plant eaten all over Southeast Asia and Bengal
Mummy	My mother, Ratnavali Baruah, who was a great cook and the daughter of Pragna Sundari Devi the writer of the ground-breaking cook book in Bengali
Pakhi	My sister, Lalitha Jauhar, from whom I learned some Punjabi dishes
Paneer	Another name for 'channa' or cottage cheese
Paratha	Handmade Indian shallow fried bread
Pulao	Also known as Pilau. A rich rice dish
Rasam	South Indian sour soup and eaten as a starter
Riki	My son, Dr. Richik Ghosh; a reasonably good cook, who developed a few dishes as a student, overseas.
Roti	Chapatti or handmade, usually round, flat unleavened bread.
Rosogolla	A Bengali cottage cheese ball in syrup

Saag	Leafy green vegetable e.g. spinach
Sauerkrat	Pickled cabbage of German origin
Sambhar	A South Indian spicy lentil preparation
Sandesh	A dry Bengali confectionary sweet made mainly with cottage cheese
Singara	A pyramid shaped savoury pastry (fried or baked) usually filled with curried items. Also known as 'samosa'.
Sara	My maid, who surprised us with some of her innovations in cooking
Sembe	Swahili word meaning coarse ground maize
Sorsé	Indian mustard or 'rape' seed
Stella mashi	My mother's friend, Stella Das, and a great cook.
Sukiyaki	A dish of Japanese origin
Sushi	Any fresh raw food dish – Japanese origin
Tarkari	A dry Bengali curry
Tengri	Leg or leg bone of animals (usually goats)
Teriyaki	A Japanese cooking technique where food is broiled or grilled in a special sweet soya sauce
Thore	Soft inside of the trunk of a banana plant – a popular vegetable of Bengal (rhymes with 'more')
Tortes	Open tart or rich cake type mixture baked in a pastry case
Zucchini	A vegetable also known as courgette

ALPHABETICAL LIST OF RECIPES

Recipe	Page
Aloo Bati-Chorchori	95
Aloo Posto (Potato Poppy Seed Curry) (IV)	99
Aubergine (Begun) Kalanji	104
Bachelor's or Students' Easy Bread	186
Baked Bean Soup	158
Baking Powder Parathas	193
Basil And Tomato Soup	151
Bean Soups	154
Beet Ghonto (Bengali)	84
Beetroot Soup (III)	140
Beigli (Sesame Roll)	188
Bengali Chicken Curry	54
Bengali Chilli Fish (III)	16
Bengali Cholar Dal (Bengal Gram) (I)	127
Bengali Cholar Dal (Bengal Gram) (II)	128
Bengali Labra or Mixed Vegetable Curry	89
Bengali Vegetable Curry or Dalna	90
Black Bean Soup	155
Bora Biriani	208
Borsch Or Beetroot Soup (I)	138
Bread Rolls	187
Burmese Fish Curry	10
Cauliflower and Potato Kalia (Bengali)	82
Chanchra Or Bengali Dry Vegetable and Fish Head Curry	29
Channa Or Dry Chickpea Curry (I)	120
Chawan Musi (I)	169

Recipe	Page
Chawan Musi (II)	170
Chhola Or Whole Brown Pea Curry	119
Chicken and Corn Soup (I)	163
Chicken and Corn Soup (II)	164
Chicken Curry (I)	58
Chicken Curry (II)	59
Chicken Korma (I)	60
Chicken Korma (II)	62
Chilli Fish A La Bengal (I)	14
Chilli Fish A La Bengal (II)	15
Chinese Chicken and Noodle Soup (I)	165
Chinese Chicken and Noodle Soup (II)	166
Chinese Chicken and Vegetable Soup	167
Chinese Sour and Hot Soup	168
Coconut Brinjal	106
Coconut Fish	19
Coconut Rice	201
Cold Beetroot Soup (II)	139
Cold Cucumber Soup (I)	143
Cold Cucumber Soup (II)	144
Cold Cucumber Soup (III)	145
Cold Yogurt Soup	181
Colonial Chicken and Egg Curry	64
Corn Soup	153
Crab Curry	50
Crab Kofta Curry	52
Curried Beef and Pumpkin	76
Dry Chickpea Curry (II)	121
Dry Curry	93
Dum Mutton	65

Recipe	Page
Easy Parathas	194
Egg Parathas	195
Fish Biryani	210
Fish Jhaal – Chilli Fish (IV)	17
Fish Jhole	27
Fish Or Prawns in Coconut Sauce (II)	39
Fish Sas (Parsi Fish Curry)	12
Goan Chicken Curry	53
Goan Liver Curry	74
Green Coriander Fish Curry	21
Green Moong (Dal) Soup (From Leftovers)	160
Green Papaya Dry Curry	80
Green Pea Soup	152
Gujarati Arhar (Toor Gram) Dal	132
Gujarati Kitchri	206
Gujarati Muslim Chapattis	197
Gujarati Peas and Cauliflower Curry	83
Hilsa (Shad) with Mustard, Coconut and Poppyseed	26
Hing Aloo-Dum (Potato with Asafœtida)	100
Hodge Podge Soup	179
Hot Rolls	190
Hungarian Goulash Soup	174
Ice Box or Refrigerator Rolls	189
Japanese Rice	202

Recipe	Page
Kanchkala Or Green Banana Curry	109
Khitchri The Parsi Way	207
Khorisa (Assamese Bamboo Pickle) and Fish Curry	13
Kochusaaker Ghonto – Curried Taro (Lat. Colocasia) Greens	116
Lamb Or Beef Mince Kebabs in Yogurt	75
Lau (White Gourd) Or Vegetable Shukto (II)	87
Lau (White Gourd) With Shrimps	32
Lentil Or Dal Soup	159
Ma's Aloo Posto (Potato with Poppy Seed Paste) (I)	96
Ma's Cabbage and Fish Curry	18
Ma's Green Papaya Ghonto or Dry Curry	81
Ma's White Pumpkin (Chaal Kumra) Curry	107
Malaysian Lobster or Prawn Curry (Lobster Rendang)	30
Masala (Spiced) Fish	24
Methi Aloo (Fenugreek Potatoes)	94
Methi Paratha	192
Methisaak (Fenugreek Greens) Fry	118
Middle Eastern Chicken and Rice Soup	177
Middle Eastern Mutton Soup	178
Minestrone	137
Mixed Vegetables with Mustard and Coconut	92
Mulligatawny Soup	161
Mummy's Aloo Dum (Dry Potato Curry)	102
Mummy's Mowcha Chenchki or Banana Flower Curry	110
Mummy's Pumpkin and Prawn Curry	34
Mutton Curry	71
Mutton Korma	66
Mutton Pressure Cooker Curry or In Daab (Green Coconut)	69

Recipe	Page
Pakhi's Black Moong -- The Punjabi Style	130
Pakhi's Rajma	122
Papaya Dalna	79
Pea Kochuri	198
Piquant Green Jack Fruit (Enchore) Curry	108
Posto (White Poppy Seed) Mutton Curry	68
Potato and Poppy Seed Dry Curry (Aloo Posto) (II)	97
Potato Soup (I)	146
Potato, Cheese, Capsicum Soup (II)	147
Prawn Curry (I)	36
Prawn Curry (II)	37
Prawn Curry in Coconut Sauce (III)	40
Prawn Malad	42
Prawn Soup	173
Prawns And Tomato	43
Prawns In Coconut Sauce (I)	38
Prawns In Daab (Green Coconut)	35
Prawns or Fish in the Oven	46
Quick Easy White Bread	185
Quick Prawn Malai (Coconut Milk) Curry (IV)	41
Quick Risotto	203
Rasam	125
Rasam With Ready-Mix Powder	126
Red Bean Soup	156
Saag Meat	72
Saag Paneer	114
Sambhar (With Home-Made Mix Powder)	124
Sambhar (With Ready-Mix Powder)	123

Recipe	Page
Sheem (Broad Beans) Paturi – Bengali	85
Shrimp And Cauliflower	33
Shrimp or Fish in Banana Leaves (Fish Pāturi)	47
Shukto (I) – Bengali Starter	86
Shukto (III) As A Variation To (I) Or (II)	88
Simple Bengali Moong (Yellow) Dal	129
Simple Bread Rolls/Sticks and Pizza Dough	191
Simple Gujarati Pulao	205
Simple Japanese Soup	171
Simple Light Prawn Kofta Curry	48
Sinhalese Fish and Vegetable Dry Curry	9
Sorsé (Mustard) Fish	25
Sorse Sag (Mustard Green) Curry	117
Soup With Butter Dumplings	172
Soya Bean Soup	157
Spicy Brinjal	103
Spinach Soup (I)	141
Spinach Soup with Coriander (II)	142
Spinach With Bori	113
Steamed Fish Burmese Style	11
Steamed Mustard Prawns or Fish	44
Steamed Potatoes with Poppy Seed Paste (III)	98
Stellamashi's Sorse Aloo (Potatoes in Mustard Sauce)	101
Stock	135
Sweet and Sour Arhar (Toor Gram) Dal	131
Tandoori Roti	196
Thick Broth	180
Thick Chicken Curry	56
Thore Chenchki	111

Recipe	Page
Thore Ghonto	112
Tomato Fish	23
Tomato Soup (I)	148
Tomato Soup (II)	149
Variations of Cold and Hot Soups	182
Vegetable Paturi (Bengali Banana Leaf Wrapped Smoked Vegetable Dry Curry)	93
Vegetable Soup	136
Yahneli Kufte (Armenian)	175
Yogurt Fish	20

www.ingramcontent.com/pod-product-compliance
Ingram Content Group UK Ltd.
Pitfield, Milton Keynes, MK11 3LW, UK
UKHW020247240426
12048UKWH00027B/1656